LISTENING TO THE MIRROR
A Bible Study

by
Al Santymire

His Way Ministries
P.O. Box 20337
Castro Valley, California 94546
www.iamyahweh.org
Listening to the Mirror/Al Santymire — 1st ed.
ISBN-13: 978-0692807064 (Al Santymire)
ISBN-10: 0692807063
Library of Congress Control Number: 2016920054
Al Santymire, Daly City, CA

Dedication

This book is dedicated to Virginia Susan Brown Santymire, who profoundly and thoroughly changed my life and steadfastly kept me focused on the task of serving God. For more than 33 years she put up with all the wild ideas, endeavors, failures and mistakes of a man who was on a spiritual rollercoaster ride. As quickly as I would set off on one of my journeys Ginny was there to encourage, steer and wait. She never tired of supporting and defending me and she was usually the one who nudged me toward seeking solace from God during the down times. The amazing part is that, just like God, she accepted me as I was and just continued working to make me better. Thank you and with an eternal love I dedicate this book to the memory of my beloved Ginny, along with three other special women who have made my life more complete and rewarding.

Hettie Irene Crawley Santymire (1923 — 2013)

Virginia Susan Brown Santymire (1953 — 2005)

Angelica Maria Martinez Santymire

Elise Megni

Acknowledgements

Many people have influenced me and shaped my way of thinking and I want to honor some of them here. All of these wonderful people have helped me develop my own reading and study habits and have fed my curiosity and desire to become more intimate with my God.

First, I want to thank Momma. From infancy she took me to church, read me the Bible and taught me to pray. She got my life started on the right path.

To the church in Hollister that gave a green, but eager, young man the opportunity to preach, grow and learn.

To Jerry Campbell and the other elders of the church in Campbell for giving direction, showing wisdom and demonstrating how to live a life dedicated to God.

To the church in San Martin for enduring my growing pains, sharing their lives and becoming a big part of mine.

For hoy and Bonnie Brown for giving me a friendship that has lasted through the years, from good times to bad, through closeness and separation.

For my son, Jason, his wife Angi, and the boys (Jadon, Cason and Jonathan) and the newest addition, Larena, for teaching me that no matter how many mistakes you make, if God is involved it will turn out well.

To John and Margo Johnson who were placed into my life by God at just the right time with just the right medicine for my soul.

To Elise, the woman who is taking what has been shaped and formed, refining me into exactly what God has in mind, and helping guide me into the vision God has for our lives together.

The major reason it took more than 10 years from the time I wrote most of the book until now to publish was my lack of faith that anyone would want to read it. I had sent out more than half a dozen copies to different people over the years but received no feedback until Pastor Butch Monk, from 3 Crosses in Castro Valley, read it, and gave encouraging, positive feedback. Without this, the book would still be sitting in a directory of my computer.

And, last but not least, to my editor and encourager Rick Chavez. Without him entering my life this book would never have been published. He took the seed of faith implanted by Butch and took me by the hand and walked me through the process, encouraging me at every step. Thank you, Rick.

Now about that title. One way the Bible is to be used is as a mirror. When we look into it, we can see ourselves; the things we are doing that are good and the things we are doing that are bad; where we are achieving God's results and where we are not. The most effective way for the words of God to penetrate into our hearts is by reading them aloud. So you are encouraged to not only read God's word, but also to read it aloud and Listen To Your Mirror.

Contents

Introduction

Whenever someone decides to write a book, the author has a goal in mind for the readers. So, what are my goals and intentions? The major goal of this book is for each reader to grow spiritually into an intimate relationship with God their heavenly Father and God their Savior Jesus Christ. If you have not begun your journey into developing an intimate relationship with God — and by so doing developing an intimate knowledge of yourself and God's purpose for you — then this book is for you. If you are on that journey but are not making much progress, then this book is for you. If you are mature, confident and engaged in daily dialogue with the Lord but still seek more information, more wisdom, and an even closer relationship with Him, then this book is for you.

The beginning, middle and end of all searches for God are to be found in His words to us. We may use supplemental tools and aids but, fundamentally, the Bible provides us with our road map to ourselves, to our Lord and to our eternity. Therefore, we must learn how to read our road map and the learning process is called Bible study.

How do you study the Bible? Most of us know how to read the Bible, but how many of us have put forth the effort to learn how to study God and His word? Most of us rely on a class book or small group study guide. Or maybe on an author who wrote on a specific subject supported by a teacher leading, guiding and directing the study. All of these methods have merit and a place in our spiritual development; if they did not I would not have written this one. But there comes a time when we must put aside the ideas of men and go directly to the source, and that is one of my primary goals for you.

Have you wondered why there are 39 books in the Old Testament, not counting the Apocrypha books, but only 27 in the New Testament? Thirty-some years after the church was founded and dozens of books had been written, Paul still admonished Timothy to study the Scriptures, or the Old Testament. Is there the possibility that we have been missing something by largely ignoring the Old Testament?

The question is, how do you make sense of the Old Testament stories? Are they just historical stories, or even parables, that are interesting only to history buffs? How about all those census numbers and genealogies? Not even a mathematician or accountant could keep from falling asleep reading them. Why did God include them in the Bible? Good questions, but if you are expecting this book to answer these questions, I am sorry. However, by the time you finish this study you will have begun answering them yourself. When you read my conclusion I will offer several reasons for why God included certain sections that do not seem inherently worthwhile. This book has four additional purposes or goals.

- This book is designed to walk you through the lives of several Old Testament characters as you read their stories. This will help you develop a study method.

- By developing a study method and learning how to apply Old Testament stories to the life of Christ and New Testament truths, you will be able to answer some of your own questions. As an added bonus, you will no longer need someone else to lead you in a Bible study! Of course, we all still need to take part in group Bible studies to help increase our own knowledge and wisdom and to share what we know with others.

- You will find Jesus throughout the Old Testament. You will recognize Him in the characters and historical events. When you read an Old Testament passage it will trigger a thought of an event or teaching from the life of Jesus. You will see how Jesus Himself relates to these characters and makes reference to them.

- You will learn more about yourself. You will be able to see how God works in your life and the value God places on you. Most importantly, you will be able to answer the question, "What is God's will for my life?"

Peter, Paul, Barnabas, Phillip, Silas, Timothy, Eunice and Lydia all used the Old Testament to tell the world about Jesus. How many of us today know Jesus well enough that we can go back into the Old Testament and point out our Messiah in the lives of those who came before?

Paul says "...all scripture is useful for teaching, rebuking, correcting and training in righteousness, so that the man of God may be thoroughly equipped for every good work."[1] This is what we want to accomplish in the following chapters. The characters we will be studying lived their lives as an example for us. As we begin to see how God worked in their lives and how they reflected the Messiah to come, we also may begin to reflect the Messiah that has come and lives within us. Throughout this book Scripture will be quoted. My desire is that you will take the time to find the Scripture that is being referenced, look it up, and read it in its context. The references will be listed at the end of each chapter and Appendix B has the full list of quoted Scriptures.

We will be looking at some of the greatest people who have ever lived. We begin our journey with a man who is hardly mentioned in the Bible, except for thirteen chapters in Genesis, and yet is the closest example of Christ in the Old Testament. We will also look at the Judge, Lawgiver and Peacemaker and see how Jesus fulfilled those same roles. We will learn about a judge and prophet who the Israelites believed had outlived his usefulness and made them want to be ruled by a king. From there we look at a man after God's own heart[2]. We will be examining why he was a man after God's own heart and what it will take for us to claim that identity. We will learn more about a man who experienced the exhilaration of a mountain top experience but who immediately had to face a valley of the shadow of death experience. We will spend some time in the Psalms, studying the events that inspired them, and revisit an event in Christ's life that mirrors what happened to the Psalmist. We will also spend some time with the prophets who wrote about the Messiah and what they experienced in their personal lives by living for God and becoming swatches of the masterpiece that was to come. We will examine people who knew they were called by God for a purpose, then discovered that purpose and glorified God by living and dying to fulfill that purpose. We will also delve into scriptures that many believe originated with Christianity and others that predate Christianity by thousands of years. Then we will look at some symbols of Christ that were crucial elements to the Jewish faith. We will close by looking at the first person to be identified as a friend of God. I can think of no greater honor than to be recognized by that label: I am a friend of God.

Please take time to pray before you read and study each chapter. Ask God to open your eyes and understanding and, most importantly, open your heart. Do not let our Messiah ask this of you, "Do you not know me…even after I have been among you such a long time?"[3] As we read the Bible, Jesus is among us. But you can spend hours in His presence and still never get to know Him, much like with the people we work around. But it will be impossible not to get to know Him if you pray and ask Him into your life before, during and after your study.

During this study many of you will be surprised by the intimacy of God with His people, the practical applications for your own life, and the mirrored events of these Biblical characters and your personal history. With appetite whetted, my goal is that you will use the Scriptures to find the answers to the questions and challenges in your life. When decisions need to be made, when loneliness, confusion, and bereavement enter your life, when unbounded joy fills your soul, or when someone else needs direction and support, you will know how and where to get God's advice, comfort, fellowship and support.

All Scripture quoted throughout this book is from the New International Version (NIV) of the Bible and used by permission.

Scripture References:

[1] 2 Timothy 3:16-17

[2] Acts 13.22

[3] John 14:9

I

Joseph:

May He Add

"Now Israel loved Joseph more than any of his other sons, because he had been born to him in his old age." — Genesis 37:3

Most of us know Joseph because of the children's Bible story about the coat of many colors but his life more closely mirrored that of Jesus than any other person in the Bible. Despite that distinction, comparatively little was written about Joseph. Genesis 30:22-24 records the birth of Joseph and his life story is recorded in chapter 37 and chapters 39 – 50. The only mention of Joseph after the Pentateuch occurs in 1 Chronicles 5:2. This is an interesting passage that concerns his lineage and gives us some insight into how inheritances were given and taken away. This could be a Bible study for another day. Joseph is mentioned only three times in the New Testament; in Acts 7, Hebrews 11:22 and Revelation 7:8.

We will look at ten examples of how the lives of Joseph and Jesus mirrored each other. We will look at the Genesis passages and the New Testament passages regarding Jesus. Then I encourage you to write down an event or events in your life that are similar to those that Joseph and Jesus experienced. This exercise is meant to show you how much you truly have in common with your Savior and how you can be a light in this the world for Jesus.

Do not be afraid or troubled that you are comparing yourself to Jesus. On the contrary, take joy that you have something in common with your Savior and know that only by his Spirit living in you can this happen! So get out your Bible and your pencil and paper, say a short prayer before you begin this study, and "May These Things Be Added Unto You"[4].

Event 1

Misunderstood by family.

Old Testament — Genesis 37:5-11

New Testament — Luke 2:41-50; Mark 3:21, 31-35; John 7:2-9

Joseph was a young man who was already hated by his brothers because he was Daddy's favorite. And now these dreams! They must have thought this was nothing but insolence and pure spite on his part. In Jesus' case, what must his brothers have thought? He thinks he is the Messiah? Give me a break. He may be a goody two shoes, but a king? What a laugh if he were not our brother.

Both cases caused a loving parent to think on the events that were happening and put them in a special place in their memory. They also created division between Joseph, Jesus, and their siblings. The initial misunderstanding led to Joseph's siblings plotting to kill him. In Jesus' case, they considered putting Him away in what we would call today a mental institution. Some people picture Joseph as a slightly obnoxious teenager making a big deal of these dreams but

16

I see a young person excited about a dream and sharing it with his family. If Joseph is guilty of anything it would be naiveté. He was probably spoiled but I do not think he had mean intent. Think of a time when you were misunderstood at home, school or work and that misunderstanding led to resentment on someone's part. How did you handle the situation? How did Joseph and Jesus handle theirs?

Write down your experience; no one will be surprised if your experience is not as dramatic as Joseph's or Jesus'. Contemplate the similarities to Joseph and Jesus, the reactions of those involved, and what you have learned from the experience.

Event 2

Unjustly accused.

Old Testament — Genesis 39:6-18

New Testament — Mark 14:55-64

The phrase, "hell hath no fury like a woman scorned," could have been coined after this incident involving Joseph and Potiphar's wife and, as we find in Jesus' case, there is no enemy like a self-righteous enemy. When lust, greed, and jealousy consume someone, they are filled with hate and cannot see their own evilness and they must hurl accusations at the object of their hatred. Think of a time when you were unjustly accused of something; being late, not following up, forgetting a date or neglecting an assignment. Most of our experiences will not have the drama or danger of the Joseph and Jesus situations but can nonetheless cause fear or trepidation and

17

lead to suspicion, typecasting, and loss of faith in people. We will also see how Joseph and Jesus reacted to these injustices.

Event 3

Not guilty of any charges.
Old Testament — Genesis 39:19-20
New Testament — 1 Peter 2:21-23

In Joseph's case, being attractive became a liability. His good looks, his ability to manage and lead and his knowledge became too much for Potiphar's wife. Just as she lusted for Joseph, the leaders of Israel coveted their power and authority over the people. Both parties had to accuse the innocent to cover their own sin. In Event 2 you were asked to think of a time when you were unjustly accused; now think of a time when you were unjustly punished.

Event 4

Deserted or forgotten by benefactors and associates.
Old Testament — Genesis 40:9-14, 23, 41:1
New Testament — Matthew 26:56; Mark 14:50-52

Joseph spent two additional years in prison after being forgotten by a former prisoner whom he had helped. Jesus died on the cross while ten of his chosen twelve were nowhere to be found near Golgotha. What does it feel like to be deserted, left alone or forgotten? This could be as small as someone closing a door in front of you or going for a job interview and the interviewer forgot and left for the day. As you record your experience, take time to describe what you thought and how you felt during the ordeal.

Event 5

Reaction when first revealed.

Old Testament — Genesis 45:1-3

New Testament — Mark 16:8

In both instances Joseph's brothers and the women who visited Jesus' tomb had assumed the men were dead. When the truth was revealed to them they were terrified. Joseph's brothers were scared because they were afraid he would treat them as they did him. The women feared because their faith could still not accept the fact that Jesus had risen.

What was the reaction when you confronted someone who was spreading false rumors about you or you caught them lying, stealing or in an embarrassing situation? Was there fear? Denial? Repentance? When you revealed the wrong, how were you feeling? Most of our experiences probably centered around siblings, but many of us have had this unfortunate opportunity at work and school. When reviewing your experience, include what was going through your mind at the time. How did others respond to your reactions? Who benefited most by your confrontation? What was your motivation for confronting the individual? How long, if ever, did it take for one or both of you to "put this behind you"?

Event 6

Forgive without being asked.

Old Testament — Genesis 45:4-8

New Testament — Luke 23:32-34

Joseph's siblings had betrayed him and they were not prepared to come face to face with a brother they had assumed was dead or, at best, a slave. Joseph has led them on, but now he needs to let them know who he is and give them an answer for his strange behavior. Wow, what an answer he gave! Did you ever think when things were at their worst in your life, that was when God was most active? That He was involved with the bad things that were happening? As for Jesus, he knew what Peter was going to do and told him He had been praying for him when Peter recognized what he had done. When we are at our worst who would believe that the love of God is summed up in such a statement, "forgive them" (or, I forgive you)? But this is exactly what Joseph and Jesus did. This may take some time for you to accept and maybe longer for you to see God at work during these times. My prayer is that you continue to search and talk with God about what His plans are and how He is leading and directing your life now.

Most likely, someone has done something to hurt your feelings. What if someone had tried to kill you? How easy would it be to forgive that person? What would they have to do to earn it? But, what if they never ask for forgiveness? How did you feel when you forgave someone? How much easier is it to say "I forgive you" or "Forget it" (and not fully mean it) than it is to say to God, "I forgive as you have forgiven me"[5]? For many Christians and most non-Christians this is the hardest action God requires of us. Some religions are partly based on punishment and retribution but not forgiveness.

I want to interject a story that occurred while I was teaching a Bible class to 2nd graders. One morning our lesson was about forgiveness and I brought up the story of Jesus dying on the cross and Stephen being stoned to death. A visitor raised his hand and asked to speak with me after class. In our discussion the boy told me that he had been abused by an uncle but no one in the family believed him. I told the boy that that would probably always be the case and that his uncle would never say he was sorry, but that he had to forgive him anyway or the boy's pain would never go away. He said he did not know if he could but he would try. Two weeks later he came back, and again asked to talk with me after class. He told me that he had followed what had been taught and believed he had forgiven his uncle. We discussed how the pain, hurt and rejection would take some time to recede and that there would always be some pain when he recalled what happened. I was profoundly moved by this experience. I believe it was the Holy Spirit at work in that young boy and me. I have not been the same since and feel blessed that God used me as an instrument of healing for this young boy.

Event 7

Prepared a place for his family.

Old Testament — Genesis 46:5-7

New Testament — John 14:1-3

Think about a sick relative, an out-of-work friend, a lonely family member or a helpless soul requesting assistance. Then imagine Joseph's family moving from hardship and near starvation to the lap of luxury. Think back on a time when you were blessed with an opportunity to give food, comfort, lodging or other assistance to someone in extreme need.

Event 8

Reunited with father.

Old Testament — Genesis 46:28-30

New Testament — Acts 1:6-11, Acts 7:54-56

How joyous an occasion it was for Joseph when he was reunited with Jacob! How about for Jesus returning to heaven after having completed the job the Father had given Him to do? The angels had Him back in their presence. The saved may now begin to savor their reward!

Have you ever been separated from someone close to you for a lengthy period of time? How often did you think of that person? How sorely did you miss them? Was the separation because of a job relocation, family dispute, or just events getting between you? In relating your experience, list some of the small details surrounding your reunion.

Event 9

Those who sought to kill him.

Old Testament — Genesis 37:18

New Testament — John 7:1, 11:45-53

  I pray that you have never been, nor will ever be, in this situation but there are times when we think things could just not get any worse. Have you ever had the experience of someone who totally disliked you and would go out of their way to say or do something against you? Or, maybe there is someone in your life whom you will never be able to satisfy or make happy. Read the adjacent Scriptures in the Book of John and see how Jesus prepared Himself to face those seeking to kill Him. Would you respond likewise? Record an experience with an offender or someone you cannot seem to satisfy.

Event 10

His death resulted in salvation.

Old Testament — Genesis 37:31-35

New Testament — Acts 4:12

  Joseph did not actually die in this situation but I would like you to relate a time when you either gave up everything or were willing to give up everything for someone else. Describe the circumstances around that time and your thoughts and feelings when making the decision. Was God part of your actions, thoughts and feelings?

Please permit me to share one more experience from my life. I was working for a company that told me to do something unethical and I refused. I then realized that it would be impossible for me to work for such a company. After discussing this with my family and questioning God in prayer we decided I should quit my job. We had no savings and no new job to go to. It was early November and the industry I was in made it difficult to find work during the holidays. But just as we had counted on, God got us through the holidays and I found a new job in January. Despite appearing less than intelligent to those in the world (by quitting my job) and potentially endangering my family's well-being, we took the step together in faith and were ultimately rewarded.

GOAL:

Now that was not so bad was it? Did you learn anything about yourself? Were you able to read any of the passages aloud? Do you see how this can be an effective way of studying the Bible? Did you learn anything new about Jesus Christ or Joseph? As you read the stories did you pick up on the feelings that Joseph and Jesus had to deal with and empathize with them? The goal of this chapter is to get you started drawing correlations between your life and those we read about in the Bible, and to see that we could easily have been one of those people. We can also begin to see that God has given us examples of how to live and how not to live. By realizing this, we can understand that God can do with us what He has done with them.

When you talk to God next time, thank Him for the life of Joseph and the gift of His Spirit in your life. I also want to take this time to encourage you to pray aloud to God whenever possible and hear what you sound like to Him.

Now that you know God is alive and working in your life, let us look at some times when it did not appear that He was there, or when it seemed like He did not want the best for you.

Scripture References:

[4] Luke 12:31

[5] Colossians 3:13

II

Moses:

The Reluctant Deliverer?

"Moses thought that his own people would realize that God was using him to rescue them." — Acts 7:25

Have you ever been so excited about doing something that you could hardly control yourself? You wanted to take part in an activity or organize an event that would "knock their socks off?" Remember how pumped up you were? When you presented your idea, what was the reaction from your fellow church members, family, friends or co-workers? Did they have the same passion and vision that you did? Or, was there resistance or discouraging remarks? Was it like Paul when no one came to his support?[6] Take several minutes to offer a prayer to God, read Acts 7:20-29, and then reflect on a story about when it was apparent that the time was not right.

Before analyzing or coming to conclusions about your experience, let us turn to these Scriptures and see some examples from Christ.

Read John 2:4, 7:6, 8:20, 8:30; Matthew 26:18; and Luke 9:51. Just as the first attempt by Moses to lead the children of Israel from bondage was not the right time, Jesus had several occasions that were not the right time. Your idea or plan may not have been wrong or bad, but the timing was just not right.

Now about this chapter's title. Because of what happened forty years earlier, many assume that it was a new idea for Moses to be the deliverer of his people and that was why he felt inadequate. But after reading Acts 7 you can see that this is not true. His mother had taught Moses about the special circumstances of his birth and infancy. Moses knew he was to be the deliverer of Israel; he had the Spirit of God within him. Moses felt called to rescue his people but when he tried he failed miserably and ended up running for his life. He left the comfort and luxury of Pharaoh's home to live with the Israelites but the prophecy given to Abraham about the Hebrew people and the end of their bondage was soon to come true.

What went wrong? Why did Moses fail? Let me present two hypotheses. One, nothing went wrong. Moses needed this experience to realize that only with God's direction and direct intervention was freedom to be realized by the nation of Israel. Two, Moses did not fail, the people of Israel failed. The people were unwilling to look outside the box. The people did not like their current situation but were not that uncomfortable with it, either. Living as slaves was more acceptable than rebelling against Pharaoh and possibly being worse off than before. There also may have been some mistrust and jealousy.

Now, go back to your experience and recall what was attempted that initially looked like a failure. Why do you think it was a failure? Was the time not right? Was the leader not ready? Or were the people not ready? There was probably an enemy in the midst fighting you. This is typically the main reason people are not ready. Another is a lack of maturity. The enemy, Satan, will take on many and various images, typically related to something good and in the form of a friend or leader. He specializes in giving us an alternative method that requires little, if any, of anyone's time and resources and nothing is accomplished. Tell me if you have heard statements like these:

"Is this the right thing for us?"

"We are not big enough."

"This will cost a lot of money."

"We do not have the resources to do it right."

"It will take years to accomplish."

"It needs more planning."

"Let us form a committee to study it."

"What if we fail?"

"What if it is wrong?"

"What if it is not God's will?"

These comments may be well intentioned and proper so do not assume they are from God or Satan until you spend time in prayer. Discuss with God how you can know when the time is right. How can you know when the time is not right? If the time is not right, what has to be done to get ready? Consider these passages before praying:

- Ecclesiastes 3:1-8
- Haggai 1:7-11
- Zechariah 3:6-7
- Luke 10:1-24
- James 4:13-17
- Acts 16:6-8

Ultimately you will need to come to a conclusion and follow what you think God is telling you to do. As you grow spiritually, your confidence and your intimacy with God will grow and you will gain understanding of why something appeared to fail.

We have spent time discussing times when we wanted to do something but were prevented. Now let us look at a time when we were called to do something but we did not want to. Consider these passages first:

- Matthew 26:39-44
- Mark 14:35-36
- Luke 22:41-44
- Exodus 3:11, 13, 4:1, 10, 13

Jesus did not want to save the world by being tortured and killed but He set the ultimate example for us by doing what He absolutely did not want to do. Moses did not want to disrupt his life and endanger it for something he may no longer have believed in or for a people who had not believed in him. It took some persuasion and even anger from God to convince Moses. At times we will find ourselves submitting as Jesus did and at other times we will be like

Moses. When my mother told us to do something we did not want to do she would say, "You can do it with or without a spanking."

Sometimes we just have to do things we do not want to do. And, as Moses obeyed through discipline, so must we as we grow and develop into a person who obeys willingly like Christ.

Take some time to answer the following questions:

- How do you say no to God?
- When have you said no to God?
- What keeps you from saying yes?

GOAL:

Hopefully this chapter will be an encouragement to you. Do not let rejection or negative feedback squelch your spirit. Keep focused on God and your relationship with Him. As we read, do not let anything separate you from His love.[7] God is also persistent and He may not let you say no to Him, even when it is something we really do not want to do. When you become aware of God's will and that you have been saying no to Him, do not be discouraged or feel guilty. This is the time to rejoice that you have heard and recognized God; turn from your refusal and begin the work God is giving you to do. Then you will be obedient, just like Moses.

It may be some time, even years, before you recognize the voice of God within you. We have many examples throughout the Bible of men and women who did not hear when God began talking to them, including Balaam, Samuel and David. Instead of being discouraged, though, look forward with anticipation to the day you will hear God speaking to you. But be aware. As Elijah found out, God will probably not speak to you the way you anticipate.

Scripture References:

[6] 2 Timothy 4:16

[7] Romans 8:38, 39

III

Samuel:

Rejected By All?

"You are old and your sons do not walk in your ways; now appoint a king to lead us, such as all the other nations have." — *1 Samuel 8:5*

Rejection. We will all experience it during our lives. We talked about it some in the last chapter. It could happen in kindergarten when another kid says no to your friend request; it could be as a teenager who gets turned down for his first date: or, it could be not getting into the college of your dreams or losing your dream job. These are major rejections that can cause depression and feelings of inferiority. These rejections hurt and will be with us for the rest of our lives. The Bible is full of examples of rejection and depression and it reveals how man tries to handle the situations versus how God wants man to handle them. In this chapter we will look at rejection and depression and in Chapter Five we will take another look at an example of depression.

Our goal in this lesson is to see how God worked with one individual to show him that some rejections are not because of your own action or inaction. The story of Samuel is an interesting study. Beginning with his mother's prayer to become pregnant, to Samuel's calling by God to a leadership role over Israel, there are many illustrations of how God and man interact. We will be looking at several events in Samuel's life and parallels in the life of Christ. Then we will see how the lessons taught to Samuel can be learned to get us through times of rejection.

Samuel initially reacted very humanly; he was hurt and angry because it seemed like he had been rejected by the entire nation of Israel. Let us begin our study by looking at some instances when Jesus was rejected. We will see how Jesus reacted as well as how Samuel was directed by God to react in similar situations.

Rejections of Jesus

- Matthew 26:25
- Mark 6:1-3
- Mark 15:34
- Luke 4: 28-29
- Luke 7:33-35
- Luke 19:47
- John 6:66

How did Jesus respond?

- Matthew 5:44
- Luke 4:30
- John 20:19

Jesus got on with His life. He had a mission to accomplish and did not let these interruptions stop Him. He taught by word and example how we are to face rejection. But God did not stop by giving us a perfect example. He has also given us examples of people who failed and were imperfect, just as we are. Let us go back now to Samuel and see how God got him through his rejections and how that mirrors what Christ taught and did.

Rejections and Responses of Samuel
1 Samuel 8:6

Samuel could have very easily quit but he did not. First he prayed. Oh, if we could only follow this example faithfully! He had the leaders leave and immediately went to God. He expressed his anger and hurt and let God soothe the pain. Why do we not do that? Why is it that so many times we turn to God only after we have reacted to the rejection?

1 Samuel 12:23

But Samuel went one step further. Not only did he go to God first, he also prayed for those who had rejected and mistreated him.[8] Consider why it is so difficult for us to pray for those who have rejected us and record some of your thoughts.

1 Samuel 15:1-3

Samuel did not stop at praying for his rejecters. He worked with the one who replaced him and when he failed God, Samuel stood up to him and told him what God was going to do about his failure.

1 Samuel 16:4-5

Samuel had to face rejection again. The one he anointed as king turned from God and Samuel's instructions. Samuel was sorrowful and mourned; today we would say he was depressed. God asked him in the beginning of Chapter 16, "How long will you mourn for Saul?" Samuel needed to anoint a successor but doing so would expose him to death at the hands of Saul. Samuel was afraid and hesitant to follow through on God's commands. The merciful God showed Samuel a way out of his dilemma.

It is important to note that Samuel had one other very big rejection that may have been the most heartbreaking. His children did not follow in his footsteps. They rejected God and would not walk with Him. If you find yourself in this situation, read the entire life of Samuel, Aaron, David, Gideon, Isaac and Jacob; they each had to live with children who did not obey. From these stories gather insight on how to intellectually handle the situation, gain strength to handle the emotions of the situation and develop wisdom for how to respond to those who are rejecting you.

What will happen if you follow the examples we have discussed in this study? What are the prerequisites you must have in your life before you can follow these examples? You are strongly encouraged to take time to develop your prerequisites and write them down. Do you have a plan to acquire them or do you even know how to put together a plan? Your plan may include examining the amount of time you spend reading and studying God's Word, in prayer, in church activities, in personal witnessing, in hospitality, in giving of time and money and in sharing with others any or all of the items in this list. Remember to talk to God before and during this activity.

You are encouraged to recall a time when you have been rejected. List your feelings at the time and make note of your reactions. If you did not follow the example of Jesus and Samuel, is there the possibility you may now follow that example to heal this rejection?

GOAL:

Rejection and heartbreak will come but you have begun to equip yourself to endure and persevere. When you turn to God first upon rejection and heartbreak, you can be sure He will be there to comfort you.

Close out this chapter in prayer and discuss with God how He worked with Samuel and how He is working with you. Talk to Him about developing the attitude of Jesus toward those who reject you. If you are not sure how or what God is doing for you, ask Him and ask for His Spirit to open your eyes of understanding and wisdom.

Scripture Reference:
[8] Luke 6:28

IV

David:

A Man After God's Own Heart

"When King David heard all of this he was furious." — 2 Samuel 13:21

Have you found the Scripture that says David was a man after God's own heart? Have you said a prayer before beginning this chapter?

I have always wondered exactly what this statement meant: a person after God's own heart. What kind of person is this? Always composed? Always gentle? Always forgiving? Never offensive? Passive? Quiet? Always right? Knowledgeable about everything? Some of these, all of these?

As I prepared for this section, one word kept coming back to me to describe a person after God's own heart. I trust you will come up with the same description that I have. Let us look at some Scriptures, examine what they are describing, put them together and see if we can conclude what it means to be a person after God's own heart. These are just a very few of the examples we are given of David and Jesus showing us God's heart.

- 2 Samuel 12:16 and Luke 13:34 and John 11:33 — exhibit anguish and grief
- 2 Samuel 13:21 and John 2:13-17 — display anger and, to a point, rage
- 2 Samuel 9:1 and Mark 10:16 — show kindness
- 2 Samuel 14:33 and Matthew 9:1-2 — are examples of forgiveness
- 1 Samuel 20:41-42 and John 13:23 — teach us to have deep affection for one another
- 1 Samuel 17:28-29 and John 14:9 — exhibit annoyance or rebuffing an insult or insinuation

Grief, anger, love, annoyance, joy and forgiveness. If you combine all these attributes into one you will describe a person with PASSION!

God is a passionate God. He is full of emotion. He does not just sit on a throne passing out impartial, uninvolved justice. He is not a judge who only weighs the evidence; He is a God who has decided to love us. Not just love us but give up everything in paradise for us. This is a PASSIONATE GOD!

This is a God who is so passionate for you that He sent His Son Jesus to die for you. He has brought loving people into your life who have made the decision to love you, be your friend and support you.

First John tells us that God is love and light. Jesus says, "I am the way, the truth, and the life"[9]. Join in a discussion with your small group about the many different terms we use to describe God.

40

If you go to Vine's Expository Dictionary or Strong's Concordance, you will find that the primary definition of the word passion is suffering, especially that of Jesus Christ; thus the reason we call the week before Easter Passion Week. In today's usage, Webster's New World Dictionary lists six different meanings for the word passion but it is most often used in one of two ways: extreme, compelling emotion; or, the object of any strong desire or fondness.

Passion in this study is "extreme, compelling emotion." What more encompassing description of God's love for us is there than this, "even while we were yet sinners Christ died for us.[10]" Even when I lie, swear, am unthankful, fail to pray or read His word, am mean, neglectful, vengeful, hurtful, antagonistic, selfish, gossipy, reckless or lazy He will jump at the opportunity to remind me I am forgiven and He gives me another opportunity to make it right. But God will also zealously correct me if I am not repentant or if I fail to recognize the wrong I have done.

This is a God who is an impassioned God and one who is compassionate beyond human capability. PRAISE GOD and may I be a man "after God's own heart."

There are times when the passionate will feel all alone. Because of their passion and zeal they may feel disconnected and assume that they are the only one wanting to reach out and strike Satan. In the next chapter we will examine this feeling of loneliness that may be why many Christians are not as passionate for God. They have a fear of isolation or of being ostracized for being different or making themselves vulnerable to the pain Satan can inflict.

Listed here is a selective list of emotions you will find ascribed to our passionate God in the Bible. How many can you add to the list?

Anger

Old Testament — Exodus 4:14, Numbers 11:33, Joshua 23:16, Judges 3:8, 1 Kings 14:15, Isaiah 5:25, Jeremiah 14:15, Ezekiel 23:25

New Testament — Mark 3:5, Romans 2:8

Affection

Old Testament — Deuteronomy 7:7

New Testament — 2 Corinthians 7:15, Philippians 1:8

Joy

Old Testament — Lamentations 2:15

New Testament — John 15:11, John 17:13, Hebrews 12:2

Sorrow

New Testament — Matthew 26:38, Mark 14:34, Luke 22:45

Desire

Old Testament — Psalm 51:6, Song of Solomon 7:10

Compassion

Old Testament — Exodus 33:19, Judges 2:18, Nehemiah 9:19, Psalm 119:77, Isaiah 54:8, Hosea 11:8, Micah 7:19

New Testament — Matthew 14:14, 2 Corinthians 1:3, James 5:11

Forgiveness

Old Testament — Psalm 130:4, Jeremiah 5:1, Jeremiah 31:34

New Testament — Acts 8:22, Colossians 3:13, Hebrews 8:12

Troubled

New Testament — Matthew 26:37, John 11:33, John 12:27, John 13:21

Peace

Old Testament — Judges 6:24, 1 Kings 2:33, Isaiah 9:6, Ezekiel 34:25

New Testament — John 14:27, Romans 15:33

Patience

Old Testament — Nehemiah 9:30, Isaiah 7:13

New Testament — 1 Timothy 1:16, 2 Peter 3:9, 2 Peter 3:15

GOAL:

You are encouraged to research other emotions and actions of God that exhibit His passion for His creation. You are also encouraged to become involved in God's kingdom with a passion for

43

saving the lost and supporting the elect. You are also challenged to look at your emotions, find corresponding examples of God or His people who exhibit those emotions and study the reactions by all who were involved.

Scripture References:

[9] John 14:6

[10] Romans 5:8

V

Elijah:

Standing Alone

"…I am the only one left…" — *1 Kings 19:10*

Why do you suppose the nation of Israel revered Elijah? We only have five recorded miracles attributed to Elijah but his successor, Elisha, presided over many more. Elijah stood up to an evil king but so did many other prophets. So it was not what he did that necessarily made him great, even though the miracles he was associated with were monumental. It was not how or when he prophesied that distinguished Elijah from the other prophets. And, we know that it was not the claim that Elijah made in 1 Kings 19, because he was set straight by God about that.

So what made Elijah so great that he was one of only two men who came to comfort and encourage Jesus on the Mount of Transfiguration? What made Elijah so great that John the Baptist is said to be the second Elijah? Where else in the Bible is Elijah talked about besides First and Second Kings and the story of the transfiguration? And, how do we see Jesus, and ourselves, in Elijah? First, let us go to the Bible and look at some events in Elijah's life that compare to events in Jesus' life.

45

Elijah	Jesus
1 Kings 17:7-16	Matthew 15:21-28
1 Kings 17:17-24	Luke 7:11-17
1 Kings 17:1-6	Matthew 23:1-36
1 Kings 19:19-21	Matthew 10:1-4
1 Kings 19:1-5	Matthew 26:36-44
2 Kings 2:1-12	Acts 1:1-9

We have stories of Elijah and Jesus each saving the non-Jew and raising a widow's dead son. There is more than one instance of both Elijah and Jesus defying and condemning the authorities of the day. Both chose the men who were to carry on their ministry.

Neither man wanted to face the consequences of his opposition to the authorities and both were carried, alive, into heaven. So what made Elijah so great in the eyes of the Israelites? Raising the dead, defying a wicked king and queen, overpowering a heathen god and exposing his powerlessness, and, maybe most importantly, he did not suffer death.

Since we cannot raise the dead and it is ever so unlikely any of us will be singularly carried into heaven, how can we be encouraged by our likeness to Elijah? When we teach the lost the Word of God, we are carrying on Elijah's work. When we stand up against religious or secular leaders because of their disobedience to God, we are carrying on Elijah's work. When we do not want to face the consequences of our actions, but ultimately trust God and accept His will, we are following in the likeness of Elijah. When we have decided that no force on this earth can separate us from God[11] and that the only authority we bow to is Jesus Christ, then we are living like Elijah. When we disciple others to follow the Lord and teach them His ways, we are following in the footsteps of Elijah. And when our life on this earth is over and we are abiding in heaven, we will be living with Elijah.

There was a time when Elijah thought he was all alone in defense of Jehovah. There are times when we feel all alone and even forsaken by God. Let us read the story of Elijah coming down from his "mountain top experience" to experience the lowest point in his life. Read 1 Kings 19:1-18. Verses 1-9 show us how pitiful we can become when we believe we are all alone. Today we would say Elijah was depressed. It is in verse 10 where Elijah tries to justify his depression and even after God reveals himself, Elijah is still wearing the mantle of self pity through verse 14. But God knew how to snap Elijah out of his depression, and that means He knows how to snap us out of ours. The key for Elijah and for the rest of us is that we must be willing to turn from our depression and turn to God, and get BUSY! God put Elijah to work and gave him a mission. God gave Elijah hope but before He could help Elijah, the prophet had to do two things: listen and get ready. To complete his mission, he had to have hope, he had to listen and he had to get ready for what was to come. So must we.

Are you listening for God or to God? Are you expecting a cataclysmic revelation (for God) or a gentle whisper (to God)? Are you looking for a place to die or a place to live?

GOAL:

Be like Elijah! Be like Jesus! Ask God how he wants you to live. Ask God what your mission is and be ready to listen to a whisper. Unfortunately, this is easier said than done, so be ready to spend a lot of time in prayer and reading. Be ready to bear up under some severe self-scrutiny. Be willing to move and make changes because God may have plans for you that you cannot even conceive.

Scripture Reference:

[11] Romans 8:35

VI

Relationships

"...Then the righteous will gather about me because of your goodness to me." — Psalm 142:7b

When exploring the subject of relationships we typically choose the topics of husband/wife, parent/child, siblings or "how to improve relationships" for our study. In this lesson we will not be looking at personal relationships between people, per se, but the type of relationships we have with family, co-workers, other church members or more casual friends. We will look at four relationships that require us to endure or face situations that will cause discomfort or pain. The last relationship we will look at is our relationship with God.

Our examination will be to read a Psalm that describes an event in the psalmist's life, the event when and how it happened, and a correlating event in Jesus' life. We will examine the passages using five criteria: a petition concerning an event, the status of the event, the action of the event, the result of the actions taken and the reaction to the results. You have the opportunity to add a fifth column to the chart, and that is describing how you respond to a similar situation in your life.

Psalm 72 - The Testers

There seems to be someone in each of our lives who has been assigned the mission to test us. Whether it be a friend or classmate, a co-worker or boss, a parent or a child they seem to question everything we do, say and think. Testers can be antagonistic or inquisitive. The way we respond to either of them will be the same. Let us look at our examples.

Psalm 72 discusses the relationships of foreign leaders with Solomon and was written after the Queen of Sheba's visit to the king. Read 1 Kings 10:1-9 and take notice of two facts. Verse one makes clear that the queen came not to test Solomon's wisdom, wealth or power, but his faith. Secondly, we observe how Solomon handled the tests from the queen. Go back to review Psalm 72 and see how Solomon perceived the relationship and the testing.

In verse one of Psalm 72 God is asked to give the king justice and righteousness. Verses 2-14 describe how the king interrelates with his people and with foreign leaders. Verses 15-17 continue the petition to God that the king be successful. The psalmist closes in verses 18-19 with praises to God because it was God who really passed the test.

Now let us look at a similar situation involving Jesus. In Luke 20:20-40 the Lord is put to the test twice. This passage shows how Jesus interrelated with those who came to test Him. In the first test He requires men to give honor to God. In the second He requires man to enter the Kingdom.

Let us make a chart to show the parallels.

Petition

Psalm 72	God is asked to grant justice and righteousness
1 Kings 10:1-9	The king is granted justice and righteousness
Luke 20:20-40	Jesus is justice and righteousness

Status

Psalm 72	Even a great king answers to God
1 Kings 10:1-9	Acknowledged as a great King
Luke 20:20-40	Acknowledged as a great teacher

Action

Psalm 72	Put to the test as a judge to measure justice and righteousness
1 Kings 10:1-9	Put to the test to measure God's wisdom and knowledge
Luke 20:20-40	Put to the test to challenge His wisdom and knowledge

Result

Psalm 72	Made righteous by his decisions
1 Kings 10:1-9	Praised for his answers
Luke 20:20-40	Praised for His answers

Reaction

Psalm 72	God given praise and honor
1 Kings 10:1-9	God given praise and honor
Luke 20:20-40	God given praise and honor

The situation with Solomon was a onetime event but it lasted for a period of time. Jesus' testing was for his entire three years of ministry. Your testing periods will vary depending on their degree, your tester and your response to the testing

Psalm 142 – The Distressed

In the first example we were being tested. In this example we are in distress. When we are in distress God will send others into our lives to help bring us out of our situation. If we avoid the relationships and withdraw, we may enter the downward spiral of depression. Thus, we have to face relationships even when we really do not want to.

The psalmist begins by voicing his own distress. As he cries out for deliverance from his predicament, God answers. But, wow, how did God answer! He sent those who were in distress, discontented and in debt and who were crying out to God for help. What a way to answer prayer! So when you are in distress and cry out to God, how do you think He may answer your prayer? Let us go to our chart.

Petition

Psalm 142	Asks for mercy
1 Samuel 22:1-5	Provided a cave
Matthew 4:23-25	Surrounded by a crowd needing mercy

Status

Psalm 142	Asks for someone to care for him
1 Samuel 22:1-5	The distressed are drawn to him
Matthew 4:23-25	His disciples answer His call (v.22)

Action

Psalm 142	Made righteous by those around him

1 Samuel 22:1-5	He is their leader
Matthew 4:23-25	Their leader; makes those around Him righteous

Result

Psalm 142	Asks for a refuge
1 Samuel 22:1-5	Provided with a forest
Matthew 4:23-25	Provides the suffering a refuge

Reaction

Psalm 142	God given praise and honor
1 Samuel 22:1-5	God given praise and honor
Matthew 4:23-25	God given praise and honor

Is it not amazing that when we get distressed we cry out to Jesus, though He could have had every reason to be one of the most distressed humans to ever live. What an example!

Psalm 52 – The Disconsolate

An even stronger feeling than distress is to be disconsolate, to grieve to the point of your heart breaking. One of the overpowering causes of disconsolation is guilt. Guilt has the power to disable you and the self-punishment can literally paralyze you.

How would you feel if a family was killed because of something you asked their father to do for you? What would you do if one of the family members escaped and came to you with the story? What would you say to God? Describe your feelings. How do they compare to David's?

In somewhat of a departure, we will look at what Jesus tells us to do when we are disconsolate and see how David used those teachings to give solace to the disconsolate.

Petition
Psalm 52	Recognize evil
1 Samuel 22:20-23	Doeg, an evil man
Matthew 11:28-30	The world
John 15:18-16:4	

Status
Psalm 52	Evil appear to be might
1 Samuel 22:20-23	Killed a priest and his family
Matthew 11:28-30	Will persecute and kill
John 15:18-16:4	

Action
Psalm 52	Trust in God
1 Samuel 22:20-23	Trust in David
Matthew 11:28-30	Trust in Jesus
John 15:18-16:4	

Result
Psalm 52	God will bring down the evil
1 Samuel 22:20-23	Safety
Matthew 11:28-30	Rest for your soul
John 15:18-16:4	

Reaction
Psalm 52	God given praise and honor
1 Samuel 22:20-23	God given praise and honor
Matthew 11:28-30	God given praise and honor
John 15:18-16:4	

Psalm 57 – The Pursued

We are pursued when someone is nagging us, continually reminding us of something we did or did not do or trying to get us to do something we do not want to do. Or, it may be, as we studied in an earlier chapter, when someone wants to do us harm. We are being pursued and, whether we want to admit it or not, there is a relationship between the pursuer and the pursued. We are given examples of how to respond when we are being pursued.

David begins by begging God for mercy. The psalmist is being pursued around the country by Saul who will kill him if he catches him. For most of Jesus' ministry the leaders were also trying to find ways to kill him, and twice he had to find a way to escape.

Petition

Psalm 57	Asks for mercy
1 Samuel 23:15,25; 24:2, 21-22	Gave an oath to Saul
Mark 3:6-7	Surrounded by a crowd intent on
Luke 4:28-30	killing Him
John 7:30	

Status

Psalm 57	Asks for someone to care for him
1 Samuel 23:15,25; 24:2,21,22	Provided with a stronghold
Mark 3:6-7	Walks away from would-be killers
Luke 4:28-30	
John 7:30	

Action

Psalm 57	Enemy unsuccessful
1 Samuel 23:15,25; 24:2,21,22	Saul went home
Mark 3:6-7	Withdrew with His disciples
Luke 4:28-30	
John 7:30	

Result

Psalm 57	Remaining steadfast to God
1 Samuel 23:15,25; 24:2,21,22	Respite from being pursued
Mark 3:6-7	Respite from being pursued
Luke 4:28-30	
John 7:30	

Reaction

Psalm 57	God given praise and honor
1 Samuel 23:15,25; 24:2,21,22	God given praise and honor
Mark 3:6-7	God given praise and honor
Luke 4:28-30	
John 7:30	

Psalm 30 – The Devoted

There are certainly people we are devoted to and throughout our life we will meet others who are devoted to us. Do not feel uncomfortable with this word or put so much emphasis on it that your understanding is more of self-enslavement than devotion. A devoted person is simply someone who holds you in high esteem and considers you a mentor and who does not doubt you.

Describe a person whose life is devoted to God. Describe a congregation whose members are devoted to God. Describe a country whose citizens are devoted to God.

Petition

Psalm 30	God delivers
1 Chronicles 22:17-19	Is God with you?
John 14:15-21	God is with us

Status

Psalm 30	Rejoicing
1 Chronicles 22:17-19	Are you at rest?
John 14:15-21	We are at peace

Action

Psalm 30	God's favor lasts a lifetime
1 Chronicles 22:17-19	Will you devote your heart and soul?
John 14:15-21	God is devoted to us

Result

Psalm 30	Turned wailing into dancing
1 Chronicles 22:17-19	Begin a sanctuary for God
John 14:15-21	God lives within us

Reaction

Psalm 30	God given praise and honor
1 Chronicles 22:17-19	God given praise and honor
John 14:15-21	God given praise and honor

In every one of these situations there are two underlying themes. Compassion for the other person in the relationship and patience that God will be involved and lead you in your actions and reactions with this person or persons. By being able to include these characteristics into your actions and reactions you will be giving praise and honor to God.

GOAL:

As you made your way through this study, did you remember to keep the theme of this lesson in mind? It is about the relationships we have with one another, especially with family. One example describes Timothy's relationship with his mother and grandmother[12]. Most importantly, this lesson is about our relationship with God. Review this lesson and see how you can use this study to strengthen all of your relationships.

Scripture Reference:

[12] 2 Timothy 2:15

VII

Hosea:

Facing Reality

"There is no faithfulness, no love, no acknowledgment of God in the land." — Hosea 4:1b

Until I began writing this chapter all of my attention on the Book of Hosea had been given to the first and third chapters. But now I see that all fourteen chapters of the book bring out the reality facing both Israel and us.

Hosea was written to shake up the people of the time. It was written to convict the guilty and to encourage them to repent and to fully illustrate God's love and forgiveness. This is a potent message for us today. We could reword Hosea 6:6 to fit our societal structure this way: "For I desire mercy, not an offering, and acknowledgement of God rather than a big check." One of God's mysteries in the Bible is being able to interpret what he says throughout the Old Testament and apply it to our daily lives. Let us look at what applications Hosea has for us.

Hosea is a book of realities. We will look at four selections from Hosea and corresponding selections from the gospels. Then we will 'interpret' these Scriptures and learn how they apply to our daily lives. I strongly encourage you to read the entire book of Hosea in one sitting in order to understand the flow and see the entire message. Then you will see how pertinent this book is to us today and also see one of the underlying reasons why the leaders in Jesus' day hated Him as they did. And, heed the warning that says, "if the world hates Jesus, it will also hate his followers."[13]

First, let us look at Hosea and the 'big picture' that is painted for us.

Men, how would you feel and react if there were rumors and strong evidence that your children were not yours, but belonged to other men due to your wife's infidelities? Then, after the third child entered pre-school she deserted you and the children to go live with a junkie and became a prostitute to feed his habit. Would you still love her? Would you want her back? In Hosea 3 God tells Hosea to get his wife back from the world of prostitution. For our modern story it would be the equivalent of you buying several fixes for your wife's junkie, packing up her things from his place, and taking her back home with you. Then the clincher: God tells you to LOVE her!

This is exactly what God has done for us. Actually, He has done this for man since the first sin. He epitomized His love in the man of Jesus when He died as payment to bring us home from our life of prostitution. God does this every time we willingly disobey Him and turn to another god. For some of us it is a daily occurrence. Remember your feelings when we described the unfaithful mate, then imagine what we put God through and how he feels. It makes me feel shame, then it makes me feel unworthy, but finally it makes me feel special and loved!

- In John 10:11, 14-16, and 26 we read of the Good Shepherd. Now read Hosea 4:16. When Jesus made the statements in verses 11-16 the leaders understood what he was saying from the Psalms. When he made the statement in verse 26 they understood him from Hosea. It is time to grit the teeth and answer: are there ever times in your life when you are rebellious, when you want to do what you want to do? Not what you are told to do or what you are supposed to do. When you go and do what you want to do you are acting just like the Israelites, just like the leaders in Jesus' time, and just like John Mark[14]. You are prostituting yourself, serving other gods, and turning away from the true God. You refuse God's pasture and are no longer His and then there is no longer a sacrifice that can be offered to atone for your wrong[15]. You must rely on God searching for the lost sheep to bring you back into pasture.

- In Luke 23:28-30 Jesus is being led out to be crucified when He turns to the wailing women and quotes Hosea 10:8. What are Hosea and Jesus telling us in these Scriptures? When you are faced with all your sins and realize what your redemption has cost and recall all those you have influenced for evil you will want to cry out to the mountains, "Cover us" and to the hills "Fall on us". Your guilt will be so great that you will be too ashamed to look upon God. When we get to this point we are often taught to ask God to forgive and then get on with a new life. The picture painted in Hosea is somewhat different and calls for our existing life to be dismantled, uprooted and purified. This is not an instantaneous event. We must address each of our wrongdoings and turn away from them completely. We must make restitution whenever possible and accept the consequences of those we cannot make right. So just as we spent so much time building a life away from God, we must begin living a life that will restore us to God.

- In Matthew 27:62-64a the leaders of the time were not only quoting Jesus' words, but also Hosea 6:2. Our revival is now possible and our cleansing and purifying can begin. It took three days of death for my God to cleanse me of my sin. It took His returning to life to give me the hope and courage to accept His forgiveness and begin my new life in Him. Unfortunately many of us are like the Israelites in Hosea 6 who God describes as "like the morning mist" and like "dew that disappears." Quickly, God's love and sacrifice is forgotten by the people. For some it is as quickly as walking out of the church doors on Sunday morning. For others it is when the first temptation is confronted and given in to. This warning is to them and to the faithful to be steadfast in your love to God!

- In Luke 15:11-32 we have the story of the lost or prodigal son with the parallel being Hosea 2:5-7, 21-23. It amazes me how little of what Jesus taught was new. We have made this point before in these studies, but I want to reinforce it here. The more we study the Old Testament the more we see of Jesus, the Light of the World[16]. Does this also help us believe that the God of Abraham, Isaac and Jacob is our God? That He is the same yesterday, today and tomorrow? Here is a parable that Christianity has embraced as its own, but which had its parallel written 750 years earlier.

The Book of Hosea helps us face reality. Our lives of sin are painted very darkly and are very ugly. But this is the truth. Our deeds are deserving of death; instead we are given righteousness. Since you have received heaven, how can you turn away? How can you not want to learn more about this God who has given all of Himself for you? Thank you God for Hosea and for helping me face the reality of my life with and without You. Amen.

"Who is wise? He will realize these things. Who is discerning? He will understand them. The ways of the Lord are right; the righteous walk in them, but the rebellious stumble in them"[17].

GOAL:

If we have not been facing reality; if we have been putting off a painful situation; if we have wanted things to be like they were or stay like they are we must now begin to look reality in the face.

To help us we will look at a familiar figure, but do so in a different light, one you may not have considered before. You may be surprised at what we can learn from our next example.

Scripture References:

[13] John 15:18

[14] Acts 13:13

[15] Hebrews 10:26

[16] Matthew 5:14

[17] Hosea 14:9

VIII

Samson:

Faith, Prayer and the Spirit

"And what more shall I say? I do not have time to tell about Gideon, Barak, Samson, Jephthah, David, Samuel and the prophets, who through faith conquered kingdoms, administered justice, and gained what was promised; who shut the mouths of lions, quenched the fury of the flames, and escaped the edge of the sword; whose weakness was turned to strength; and who became powerful and routed foreign armies." — Hebrews 11:32-34

Samson is most known for his relationship with his wife, Delilah. But for this lesson we want to deal less with his exploits with women and his physical prowess and more about why he was inducted into Faith's Hall of Fame. When we read the account of Samson in the Book of Judges we are not given many indicators that Samson had an overabundance of faith, especially since he kept chasing after Philistine women.

Like so many other accounts in the Old Testament, many parts of the stories are left untold. Fortunately, the New Testament points us back to these stories with some revelation that makes us take a different look and gain a different perspective on what is happening. Such is the case with Samson. If it were not for the passage in Hebrews we could, and most likely would, draw the wrong conclusions about the man.

By looking at Samson as a man of faith, what he did and how he accomplished it takes on a new meaning. By realizing that Samson was also a man of prayer rounds out this new man who we are seeing, and lo and behold we can see Jesus through him!

Let us look at four parallel Scriptures between Samson and Jesus. We will see the similarities in their births, how prayer was integrated into their lives, how the Spirit filled their lives and how they sacrificed their lives for their people.

Samson had an angelic birth announcement when, not only did an angel appear to Samson's mother, but also to his father. Judges 13:2-24 gives us the story of how the birth of Samson came about. Compare that Scripture with Luke 1:26-38 and Matthew 1:18-25. The mothers first, then the fathers, were spoken to by the angel. Both conceptions were miraculous, one of a sterile woman and one of a virgin girl. All four parents obeyed the words of God and both sets of parents raised their boys according to God's wishes.

Judges 13 ends with verse 25 and the stirring by the Spirit. At some point in Samson's early manhood the Spirit began directing his life. In Luke 4:14 we read of a similar account about Jesus. Both men, filled with the Spirit, begin working on the plan God has laid out for them to accomplish. Samson's calling was to break the stranglehold of the Philistines over the Israelites, and Jesus was sent to break the stranglehold of sin on mankind.

In the Book of Judges we see two prayers from Samson. In Judges 15:18-19 notice the assuredness that he would be given water. Imagine saying these words to a friend, "Are you going to give me something to drink or will I have to die of thirst?" The person asking the question is indeed in need of a drink, but the person is also just as sure that he will be given something to drink, and dying of thirst is never an option. This is another evidence of Samson, the man of faith. The second prayer, in Judges 16:28, is more formal. Samson knows he fell short of what God expected of him but he also knew that God forgives and would grant him one more request. How do we know he trusted God to answer his prayer? He pushed the pillars aside and the building came down, did it not?

All men of faith have a strong prayer life and we have many examples of Jesus praying. Let us look at one in Mark 1:35 and the other in Mark 6:46. These two passages show to what lengths Jesus had to go in His prayer life and highlight the fact that the recorded accounts of His actual prayers were but a very small part of his prayer life.

While it may appear that we are privy to very few prayers offered by the men and women of the Bible (only two from Samson), nearly every hero in the Old Testament has recorded at least one of their prayers. Visit the Book of Acts in the New Testament and count the number of prayers offered to God.

Many consider the ultimate sacrifice that of giving up your own life for someone else. In Judges 16:29-31 we read the final account of Samson. In verse 28 he had said "get revenge…for my two eyes." Was Samson making this personal? Was this what his life came down to or is there more to this request than meets the eye? Why had Samson lost his sight? Sin. What was Samson wanting to avenge? Sin. Not only his sin, but also the sins of the Philistines. He knew that he was going to die because of his sin. But the Philistines also needed to be punished for the sins they committed against him and Israel. Just as Samson had to die for his sins and those of the Philistines, Jesus had to die for ours and Samson's. I have included as an addendum the story of Jesus' last night on earth, including His death on the cross. The addendum in Appendix A combines the four gospel accounts into one story to give the full impact of the events during that 18-hour period.

Now let us tie everything together. We are to be a people of faith, filled with the Spirit[18] and prayerful. By rereading the Samson account with the awareness of his faith and Spirit-filled life we can see how his life mirrored at least a portion of the life of Jesus. We can see how God wants us to talk to Him, at times with a familiarity that Samson exhibited, other times with a spirit of humility and repentance, and when we want God to punish sin. We see those same traits in Jesus' life and we should see them in our own.

Jesus lived a perfect life. Samson did not live a perfect life, nor can I. But through the life of Samson I can see how a man, who could not overcome his desire for beautiful women, could be forgiven by God and be used to accomplish God's purpose. God is much more interested in where your heart is than what you accomplish or fail to accomplish and that is why we need to be people of faith and prayer who are filled by the Spirit.

GOAL:

Each reader will determine to fill their life with faith, prayer and the Holy Spirit. You may want to set goals or put together an action plan to help hold yourself accountable.

Scripture Reference:

[18] Ephesians 5:18

IX

Jeremiah:

The Empathic Prophet

"My heart is broken within me; all my bones tremble. I am like a drunken man, like a man overcome by wine; because of the Lord and his holy words." — Jeremiah 23:9

Jeremiah is generally known as the "Weeping Prophet." When he began his work as a prophet he was preaching that a reformation of Israel was needed. In the nation, there was a growing confidence that God would never allow His throne to be overtaken and Israel did not want to hear of doom and gloom. All was well! But then there was Jeremiah lamenting over the future that surely was not to be.

Jesus had a similar message. Changes must be made or destruction awaits. As with Jeremiah the message was to the heart, not about the outward appearance. Israel was tearing down its idol shrines. The Torah was being read in the synagogues again and all was well. The people and leaders were following the teachings of the rabbis, Israel had its own government and was establishing centers around the world. All was well, but their hearts were far from God.

Let us look at the following three accounts in Jeremiah and Jesus' life:

Jeremiah	Jesus
Jeremiah 1:9	Matthew 3:16,17
Jeremiah 1:7-8	Luke 2:46,47
Jeremiah 1:17-19	John 14:10

Both men were filled with God's Spirit to guide them in what they had to say. Both men were led to Israel and each delivered messages the leaders did not want to hear. Both were assured that God was with them and would oversee their safety. As you read Jeremiah 9:23,24[19-25] and Jeremiah 29:11-13[26-32] we discover corresponding New Testament Scriptures. How can you apply these verses to your personal life or to the lives of your congregation, small group or Bible class? Here is a list of Scriptures related to Jeremiah. Add more to the list and know the Spirit is leading you.

Old Testament	New Testament
Jeremiah 9:23-24	1 Corinthians 3:18-23
	James 4:13-16
	Luke 12:16-21
	Romans 11:22
	Ephesians 2:7
	Titus 3:4-7
	1 Corinthians 1:31

Old Testament	New Testament
Jeremiah 29:11-13	Ephesians 1:11
	Romans 15:13-14
	Titus 1:1-2
	Luke 18:1
	Hebrews 6:17-19
	Matthew 7:7
	Acts 17:27

I want to close this chapter with a passage from *"The Representative Men of the Bible"* by George Matheson, published in 1903. He took a different view of Jeremiah and much of what he says will challenge our conventional thoughts and force us to rethink some of our assumptions about God.

"Jeremiah, then, was a mental sufferer — his affliction came from within. What was the nature of this mental suffering? The pain of the mind may have as many different sources as the pain of the body. Every feeling of the heart has its own special pain — pride, humility, anger, love, envy. What is Jeremiah's source of mental unrest? It came from the keenness of his intellectual sympathy. Intellectual sympathy [or *empathy*; my word not Mr. Matheson's] is the power to put yourself in the place of another — to feel another's experience as if it were your own. Men possess the power in vastly varying degrees. In some it seems almost absent — there are those who say, 'Am I my brother's keeper?'[33] In others it is so strong that it appears to absorb the personal life — to leave no room for the

73

individual wants. It reaches its climax in the Son of Man, in whom the identity between the sufferer and the spectator is so pronounced that He can say of the calamities of life, 'Inasmuch as they did it unto the least of my brethren, they have done it unto Me.'"[34]

"Into whose place does Jeremiah put himself? That is the final question, the crucial question. And the answer is beyond measure a startling one — he puts himself in the place of God. He tries to imagine what he himself would feel if he were God Almighty beholding the state of His creatures. He says to himself, 'If I were the Divine Being seated upon the throne of the universe and looking upon the ruin of the land I had loved so well, what would my feeling at this moment be?' He says it would be the feeling of a loving husband towards an unfaithful wife. He pours forth the love-song of a wounded heart, but he conceives it as sung by the Almighty. [Jeremiah 10] It is God's song he sings — not his own. He loses sight of his own personality. His heart breaks with the Divine burden, his spirit groans with the Divine grief. It is the most remarkable vicarious sorrow I know in the whole course of the Old Testament. Isaiah's was a vicarious sorrow; he, too, put himself in the place of another. But Isaiah put himself in the place of the people; his was, after all, the sympathy of the human with the human. Jeremiah put himself in the place of God; his was the sympathy of the human with the Divine. A phase of mind so striking demands a moment's consideration."

"We are again and again exhorted to pity the sorrows of those beneath us, in other words, to imagine ourselves encompassed by the privations of an inferior condition. But conceive the exhortation given, 'Pity the sorrows of God; try to sympathize with the cares incidental to a Divine Being!' Should we not feel the mandate to be the wildest of paradoxes? We never think of sympathy as ascending. We think of it as going down, as going round, but not as going up. To pity that which is above is a novel thing; it seems almost a contradiction in terms. Yet this is the gospel of Jeremiah, nay, this is the gospel of a greater than Jeremiah. What means the solicitation to take up the Cross of Christ? What means the exhortation to participate in the sacrifice of Calvary? What means the invitation to have communion with the body and blood of the 'Man from heaven'? Is it not simply the call to lend your human pity to the sorrows of the Divine Life — to enter sympathetically within the gates of its Gethsemane? Divested of all forms, what else than this is meant by the fellowship with Christ's sufferings? The key-note of Christianity is sympathy with God, solicitude for God, anxiety for God. Why does the prayer which teaches to pray make me begin with the Divine wants? Why does it tell me, before asking for my daily bread or even for my pardon, to say 'Hallowed be Thy name, Thy kingdom come, Thy will be done in earth as it is in heaven?'[35] It is because Christian sympathy is, before all things, sympathy with God, because the deepest shadow which presses upon the soul of a follower of Christ is a vision of the cloud which seeks to dim His glory."

"Now, Jeremiah comes very near to this New Testament picture. It is to him we owe the very phrase 'New Testament'[36]; he

75

was the first who ever used it. He was before his time. Posterity felt this — felt that he should have belonged to a later age. It is to this that I attribute the legend of after days that he rose from the dead. Men came to realize that his own age was unripe for him, and they tried to bring him further down the stream. I do not wonder. He is to my mind the most modern of the ancients. He is closer to the Cross of Christ than any pre-Christian man I know. In a more direct sense than Isaiah he is entitled to the name which Isaiah bears — 'the Evangelical Prophet.' Isaiah has more Messianic vision, but Jeremiah has more Messianic feeling. Isaiah is a humanitarian — he wants a Christ for the sake of man; Jeremiah is a mystic — he wants a Christ for the sake of God. Isaiah seeks to cleanse the earthly temple; Jeremiah desires to gladden the heavenly courts. Isaiah looks at the sorrows of men and longs for a deliverer; Jeremiah contemplates the sorrows of the All-Father and longs for a comforter[37]; Isaiah views the work of Christ as a source of peace to the struggling human heart; Jeremiah views the work of the Christ as a source of joy to the Divine Spirit. The prayer of Isaiah is the Lord's Prayer, but it is the second half — 'Give us our daily bread', 'Forgive us our debts', 'Lead us not into temptation'. The prayer of Jeremiah is the earlier trio — 'Hallowed be Thy name', 'Thy kingdom come', 'Thy will be done in earth as it is in heaven'".

"Be this my opening prayer, O Father — the prayer for Thee! Let me put Thy wants first, foremost! Ere I remember my daily bread, let me remember Thy Divine beauty! Ere I ask for my pardon, let me pray for Thy prosperity! Ere I beseech Thee for my guidance, let me wish Thee to be glorified! Hitherto, I have given all my sympathy to the wants of my brother; let me remember the wants of my Father! I have heard men say 'God is sufficient unto Himself'. Nay, my Father — for Thy name is Love[38]. Love cannot be sufficient unto itself; the larger it is, the less self-sufficient it must be. Teach me the sorrows of an infinite love in a loveless world! Help me to understand Thy cry for communion! Let me feel the solitude of being Divine when there is no heart to share the Divineness! Let me enter into the pain of my Lord — the pain of unrequited love! Let me break Thy loneliness with the touch of a kindred hand! Often have I said 'Thy kingdom come' for my own sake; let me say it for Thine! Often have I prayed 'Thy will be done' to bring my peace; let me pray it to bring Thine! Thy heart is not at rest when other hearts are hardened; Thy Spirit is on the waters when other wills are wayward. I understand Jeremiah's sorrow. I understand his pity for Thy lonely perfectness, Thy solitary greatness, Thine unshared purity. I understand his sadness for the single star of Bethlehem — alone in a boundless sky. I understand his tears over Thy heart without a home, Thy love without a lodgment, Thy revealing without response, Thine appeals without answer, Thy calls without communion, Thy cares without companionship, Thy work without watchers, Thy voice without vibration in a human soul. In my prayers, O God, let me remember Thee!"

Have you ever viewed God this way? Have you ever felt this way toward God? Have these thoughts of Jeremiah and prayer from

Mr. Matheson caused you to stop and reconsider your prayer life and how you view God? I encourage you to reread this chapter, reflect on its content, then talk to God about your feelings, Mr. Matheson's concepts and God's position on the matter.

GOAL:

My prayer for you is that this study will help bring about a lasting transformation in your life and that your relationship with God will continue to grow and become more intimate.

Scripture References:

Note: The superscripted numbers in Mr. Matheson's writings are the author's and not in the original.

[16-25] Listed above

[26-32] Listed above

[33] Genesis 4:9

[34] Matthew 25:40

[35] Matthew 6:9-13

[36] Jeremiah 31:31

[37] John 14:16 (KJV, TLB)

[38] 1 John 4:16

X

Jonah:

The Sign Men Did Not Recognize

"The men of Nineveh will stand up at the judgment with this generation and condemn it, for they repented at the preaching of Jonah, and now one greater than Jonah is here." — Luke 11:32

Jonah was a prophet during Jeroboam II's reign, who foretold of good things to come, mainly the expansion of Israel and prosperous times for the nation. He is possibly the only prophet appointed by God who did not include a prophecy of gloom and doom for Israel. Jonah was on a roll and everything was going great for him until that day when God told him to go to Nineveh. On that day Jonah's life, as he saw it, came to a crashing halt. God wanted him to go where and do what? What God was asking was just not possible. No way could Jonah do what God wanted. So the prophet did what any stubborn, self-centered, rebellious child would do: he ran away from home.

He not only told God no, but absolutely not! Jonah knew that God was going to do something great in Nineveh if He was instructing Jonah to go there and preach. Jonah just could not let this happen. Nineveh was the enemy that wanted to conquer Israel. They did not worship Jehovah. They were evil. They were not circumcised. They were foreigners. They ate unclean food in an unclean manner. They did not keep the Sabbath. They worshiped other gods. They did not recognize Jehovah as the one true God. They took what was not theirs. They were arrogant and proud. They had little to no compassion. They were ruthless.

No way! There was just no way Jonah would preach repentance to those despised people. There should be a place in Sheol reserved for each one of them, not to mention individual name tags! Jonah gave up his life, home, possessions, security and future to flee to Tarshish. If he was on the other side of the world, there was no way that the message could be preached to Nineveh. God just had to be put in His place and reminded of who His chosen people were.

The most obvious sign of Jonah was the three days in the fish symbolizing Christ's three days in the tomb. The people heard what Jesus said, but could not fathom exactly what He meant. The leaders knew what Jesus was saying but did not want to believe it. To show that they understood they put a guard at Jesus' tomb[40]. But the leaders willingly disregarded the sign of Jonah that Jesus was pointing out to them.

The most significant sign, and the one Jesus wants us to see, was their willful disobedience and arrogance. Their desires and plans were obviously more important than God's. Jonah's life, from the time he received his assignment until the end of the book, was in rebellion against God because the Lord was telling him to do something he did not want to do. Jonah wanted what he thought was right, what he had been taught was right, what he knew was right! But the leaders of Jesus' day were worse! They absolutely refused to consider that Jesus just might be who He said He was. Their rebelliousness and hardheartedness condemned them to eternal death and Christ to a death on the cross.

Now here is the crux of this lesson. What was it about Jonah that Jesus drew the people's attention to? Was it his childish behavior? No. Was it his rebellion? Indirectly. Most importantly, it was his acceptance of God's decision and doing His will. It was Jonah's doing what he was commanded to do, becoming obedient to God and submitting to His will. Jonah set aside his own will to do God's, although it took quite a bit of persuasion. In both Matthew's and Luke's accounts, Jesus draws attention to the fact that Jonah preached God's word to the Ninevites. Jesus begins His discourse on Jonah by drawing our attention to the 'death and resurrection' of Jonah and after this resurrection his preaching and Nineveh's salvation. We can all see how this is a symbol for what Christ has done for all of mankind. It was through His death, burial and resurrection that man is saved. But, it is through man's preaching that the world is made aware of salvation and that a response to God's invitation is required.

So the sign men did not recognize was that we must overcome our rebellious nature and submit to God's authority. We must be ready to accept whatever job He has for us to do. If we accept Jesus as our savior, God will work with us, be patient with us and keep giving us second chances until the good He has planned for us bears fruit. For some of us there may be times when we rebel against God. God's message from Jonah is that He will always be here for you and will continue blessing you, even though in your rebellious state you restrict the blessings God can bestow on you. How many blessings could He give Jonah in the belly of the fish? You will not receive God's full blessings until you turn from your rebellion and seek Him out. How do we see Jesus in Jonah, besides the symbolism?

- Jonah never renounced his faith in God.
- Jonah trusted God to deliver him.
- Jonah knew God would do great things through him and save Nineveh if they were given the chance to repent.
- Jonah preached the word God gave him.
- Jonah preached salvation to a lost world that was not Jewish.
- Jonah talked with God when He addressed him.

Consider these Scriptures concerning Jesus and see if you can see Jesus in this stubborn rebellious man who has given the world the sign they did not recognize.

- Matthew 12:38-42 — Matthew's account of Jesus' teaching on the sign of Jonah.
- Luke 11:29-32 — Luke's account of Jesus' teaching on the sign of Jonah.
- Jonah 1:10; Matt. 4:1-11 — Jesus never yielded to Satan and never renounced God.
- Jonah 1:5, 12, 16 — Notice the similarities between this and Jonah's time at sea: they were both asleep; they both knew

what it would take to quiet the storm; there were other lives at stake; and there was great amazement by those on the boats when calm was restored.

- Jonah 1:3, 3:1; John 2:1-5 — Some believe this was a sign of reluctance on Jesus' part to perform the miracle and begin his ministry.
- Jonah 3:4; Luke 13:3 — Repent or perish.
- Jonah 3:4,16; Matthew 15:21-28 — Jesus appears reluctant to perform a miracle but the Canaanite woman puts up a good argument and reveals her faith and Jesus heals her daughter.
- Jonah 4; John 14:16 — One example of Jesus relating a discussion He had with God

GOAL:

Acknowledge the fact that there will be times when you will run away from God, no matter how long you have been His child and no matter how strong you are in the faith. There will be those who you do not want to save or share the gospel with. There will be times when you have to confess that you have been evading God. There will be times when you have to accept the consequences of running away from God. But take courage and reassurance, knowing that God will seek you out and restore you. Your responsibility will be to listen for Him and answer Him when He calls. When you begin to do the things God has given you to do, you will need to do them trusting Him to deliver the results He wants, not the ones you want.

Scripture Reference:

[40] Matthew 27:63-66

XI

Signs And Wonders

"I myself did not know him, but the reason I came baptizing with water was that he might be revealed to Israel." — John 1:31

If you are expecting a chapter devoted to miracles and supernatural events that were recorded in the Old Testament and that Jesus likewise performed, sorry. The signs and wonders we will be focusing on are the messages in the Old Testament that we normally associate as a New Testament teaching. We have touched on this subject before but want to devote a full chapter to it.

Do you realize that Christ only made one claim of giving a new commandment? That means all the other commandments He gave us throughout the gospels had been given before. In John 13:34-35 Jesus says "A new command I give you: love one another. As I have loved you, so you must love one another. All men will know that you are my disciples if you love one another." This type of love, called agapé, is an unconditional love. It is not dependent on the recipient's accepting it or returning it. It is a decision you make to love. This is the revolutionary teaching, revealed to Israel, that has turned the world upside down. The world does not, nor cannot, understand it. As followers of Jesus, we are taught that God is love[38]. If we could only learn to love (agapé) one another, there would be no way for us not to have an intimate relationship with God. The only way the world will be turned upside down today is for each person who confesses Jesus as Savior to love the world, family, neighbor, enemy, friend and rival with an agapé love.

This is not to say that most of what Jesus taught was not new. His teachings in Matthew 6 and 7 were new to the lay person who had been taught by the rabbis all their lives, teachings which Jesus was denouncing. Jesus' style and the authority He claimed that enabled Him to teach as He did was what was new and threatening to the existing leadership.

Some may point to Jesus' teachings in Matthew 5 regarding murder, adultery, oaths, eye for an eye and love for enemies as new. But, as we read them, let us see what we find regarding these teachings in the Old Testament.

Murder and Hate

Old Testament — Exodus 20:13; Leviticus 19:17

New Testament — Matthew 5:21-22

Jesus took the words in Exodus and Leviticus and brought the teaching to a logical and spiritual conclusion.

Adultery

Old Testament — Proverbs 6:25

New Testament — Matthew 5:27-28

Again, Jesus takes the Old Testament teaching and draws the logical and spiritual conclusion and puts it into a factual commandment.

Divorce

Old Testament — Malachi 2:13-16; Jeremiah 3:8; Hosea 3:1

New Testament — Matthew 5:31-32

Simply put, God has never, nor will He ever, intend for a married couple to divorce. God's desire has been that a married couple remain together, that they become as one[41]. In the Book of Malachi God says He hates divorce; in the Book of Hosea He commands Hosea to take his adulteress wife back. In the Book of Jeremiah He grants Israel a certificate of divorce because of her adulteries. The implication was that Israel, through her blatant actions, was asking for the divorce.

Oaths

Old Testament — Exodus 20:7; Leviticus 5:4; Leviticus 19:12; Hosea 4:15; Ecclesiastes 5:4-6a

New Testament — Matthew 5:33-37

The Jews had so corrupted God's teachings that taking an oath, except a public one, could easily be broken. Christ is warning that God takes oaths seriously and that it is better for one to just let his yes be yes and his no be no (almost exactly what the writer of Ecclesiastes said more than 900 years earlier). When taking oaths becomes commonplace it is easier to make a careless oath that has dire consequences (Judges 11:31, 34, 35). Hosea warns the people about making oaths they cannot or will not honor, and invoking the Lord's name in the oath.

Eye For Eye

Old Testament — Exodus 21:24; Leviticus 24:20;

Deuteronomy 19:21

New Testament — Matthew 5:38-42

By the time Jesus gave the discourse regarding this law in the Old Testament, anyone could take "matters into his own hands" and inflict the punishments God had given only to judges to carry out. In the Old Testament, if the matter was not important enough to take to court, they did not fight over it. Jesus expounded on that theme and said, let the bully have what he wants, and then do him one better and go the extra mile or give the extra garment. That was something unexpected, and for most people something new.

Enemies

Old Testament — Proverbs 16:7; Leviticus 19:18

New Testament — Matthew 5:43-48

Jesus approached His repudiation of how the Jews were applying the law compared to God's intent by challenging their righteousness. Since you are a special people, set aside by God, why do you act like everyone else? If you love your neighbor and hate your enemy, then you are no different than pagans and tax collectors. If you hate your enemy it will be impossible for you to live at peace with him as Proverbs encourages. I cannot help but think of David and Saul while reading this and how David refused to take revenge or punish Saul. David was Saul's enemy, but Saul was not David's. A person cannot be your enemy if you love him, but you can be his.

GOAL:

What is old has become new and what is new has become old. God is the same yesterday, today and forever[42]. He loves me as He loved Adam. The message He gives me, He gave to Adam. Give praise to an unchanging, eternal God! Examine anew the spiritual lessons to be learned from Old Testament teachings and see Jesus in each of them, but almost as important, see yourself and your own spirituality in them. Let me issue a challenge: the next time someone demands something from you that they do not deserve or have no right to have, give it to them with these words, "In the name of Jesus Christ my Savior and for his glory I give you _____". How do you think the person will react? How do you think you will feel?

Scripture Reference:
[42] Hebrews 13:8

XII

Here He Is

"Here I am! I stand at the door and knock. If anyone hears my voice and opens the door, I will go in and eat with him, and he with me."
— *Revelation 3:20*

In this chapter we want to focus on Jesus and the symbolism of the Old Testament that shows us the way to Him. We will be looking, not at people, but at symbols and ceremonies.

In one sense this entire study is a preamble to the Book of Hebrews. The Book of Hebrews was written around 68-69 AD by an elderly man to a group of Christians who had endured persecution and were ready to sit back and wait for Jesus to return. We could compare them to many people over 60 today who have been in the church most, if not all, of their lives. They believed they had done their part, knew enough, and deserved a rest. In short they were tired and had lost their zest and zeal. The book goes back and draws on Scripture; the writer uses nearly 40 references to Old Testament writings. He shows them that they did not know it all, but in fact were still babies, that what they had endured was just a taste of what the patriarchs, judges and prophets had endured, and that rest only comes when this life is over.

There are several different reasons why the Book of Hebrews was one of the last books to be included in the canon, and that many people through the ages have had trouble with the book. It is not a popular study book today, maybe because deep within our souls it convicts us and shows us where we are coming up short. It challenges us to be more than what we are. It dares say that we do not know all or hardly any of God's plan. It says that what we have trouble understanding is milk or baby's food, and that we should be way past that stage in our development.

We will look at three symbols: the veil, the High Priest and the sacrifice.

Veil. Exodus 26:31-33; Leviticus 21:23; Numbers 4:5,6; Matthew 27:51; Mark 15:38; Luke 23:45; Hebrews 6:19

The veil in physical terms is easy to define and understand. But what about the spiritual? What is the meaning of the veil? Is it faith? Is it sin? Is it the Law? Is it Death? Take your pencil and paper and list your thoughts on each of these possibilities and your conclusion.

Faith _____

Sin _____

Law _____

Death _____

Conclusion _____

Many will ask, "Why do we care? It does not really make any difference. I will be saved regardless of whether I know the meaning of the veil. So, why make a big deal out of it?" If you are the one asking these questions and making these statements, I will pose several to you. Are not these the same statements you hear consistently from youth, laziness and ignorance? Are not these defensive questions trying to justify why someone does not know? If God took the time to have it discussed, should we not want to know what He means?

We should want to know because God has created this symbol for a reason. He did not just throw it in as a filler or neglect to give it a spiritual meaning. You have been given four possibilities and your own ability to reason. In your own good time during your spiritual maturation you will come to a conclusion about, and realize the importance of, this symbol.

High Priest: The High Priest was only to be a descendent of Aaron and was the only person who could go past the veil to the inside of the Holy of Holies to make the annual sacrifice for the people. The office of High Priest was the most holy position God ever gave to man before Jesus. But, as man is so apt to do, he defiled even this most holy of positions.

Many of us read the term High Priest in Hebrews and get a vague picture of a man dressed in a colorful outfit praying and blessing people. To fully understand what it means to have a High Priest, to help us see more fully the role Jesus is to play in our spiritual life, let us examine what God ordained of the High Priest.

Exodus 29 describes the ordination process of the High Priest. Exodus 39:1-32 describes the High Priest's garments.

93

Leviticus 8 describes the ordination of Aaron and his sons. Leviticus 16 describes the High Priest's duties on the Day of Atonement, the one time a year he was permitted to go beyond the veil. Leviticus 21 and 22 detail rules for the priesthood, with verses 10-15 referring specifically to the High Priest. Numbers 3 and 4 deal with the responsibilities of the Levites and the supervisory role of the High Priest. Most of Numbers 8 deals with the role of the High Priest in ordaining the Levites for their work. Numbers 19 describes the sacrificing of the red heifer for purification after being among the dead.

The High Priest was a holy position that was accompanied by some pomp and circumstance. It has a unique position in our spiritual lives as it did in the lives of the Israelites. The High Priest was never set up to be the actual physical leader of the people. He was not an elected official but he had certain duties and rites to perform. Above all, he was the intermediary between God and man. In essence, the High Priest was the only hope man had of approaching God. Without his intercession, the people appeared before God as sinners. With his intercession, they appeared white as snow[43]. Purity and the atonement of sin could only come with the sacrifice offered by the High Priest. It was the action of the High Priest that took the people from a physical being to a spiritual being and into the presence of God. We are reminded that Jesus, as our High Priest, offered Himself as the greatest sacrifice, once and for all on the cross[44].

Let us go through the Old Testament and take a look at how God used this office during its earthly institution. What is interesting about the office of the High Priest is its relative quietness. God, throughout most of the Old Testament, kept the High Priest office separate from the leadership. Eli is a good example of why. (Read 1 Samuel 2). In this manner, the office of the High Priest could remain free of corruption. This was true of most of Israel's history until about midway between the last book of the Old Testament (Malachi, circa 400 BC) and the birth of Christ. It is evident at the time of Christ that the office of the High Priest was very political, but still commanded reverence from the people. Throughout the books of Chronicles and Kings you will find reference to the High Priest (usually just titled priest) being asked to offer special sacrifices as intercession with God either in praise or repentance. Ezra, a priest himself, discusses the priests and High Priest's roles and re-establishes the worship services in Israel after the remnant had been restored. There was still a High Priest and Ezra yielded to him (Ezra 8:33). The Book of Nehemiah is interspersed with the workings of the priests and High Priest. The Book of Haggai also recounts the events that occurred during the rebuilding of Jerusalem after the captivity. Zechariah 2 and 6 relate stories of the High Priest.

Were you surprised to find out how much there is about the High Priest in the Old Testament? The people of Israel were never permitted to forget God and they were to always have an intercessor. God gives us example after example of how He is always with us and at times of joy, peace, fear, war and repentance we can come before Him through our intercessor, the High Priest, and He will hear us. By the time of Christ, the High Priest was no longer the people's intercessor. He was a political appointee carrying out the logistics of the job and heading up the governing body. Man needed a new High Priest to re-establish intercession and bring back the personal relationship God wants with man.

Sacrifice: Christ's death on the cross removed all need for blood sacrifices. Directly, His death eliminated the Passover, atonement and scapegoat sacrifices. His death occurred during Passover but our emphasis is on the atonement. I wonder how many people realize the importance and comprehensiveness of this one sacrifice. The Jews needed three sacrifices to be free and forgiven. Passover freed them from slavery to man and atonement washed them of their sins. The scapegoat carried their sins away but the Jews had to do this every year. This first covenant with man required both sacrifice and obedience. Jesus' sacrifice was once and for all. It fulfilled or completed the first covenant with God and man. It opened up a new covenant where sacrifice was no longer required of man. Man's obligation to God is to obey. For us to fully appreciate Jesus' sacrifice let us examine some of the rituals man was required to perform under the first covenant.

The Passover was first instituted in Exodus 12. The first seven chapters of Leviticus discuss the different offerings and sacrifices the Israelites were required to offer. Chapters 12-15 describe other rituals required for cleansing and atonement. Chapter 16 describes the Day of Atonement required of the Israelites in the desert. Chapter 23 describes how the Sabbaths are to be followed on Passover and the Day of Atonement. In Numbers 9 we are shown a situation where some people were unclean and could not celebrate the Passover without Moses going before God to ask for a special directive. This shows us how restrictive and limited the sacrifices were under the first covenant. Numbers 28 introduces the additional requirement of an atonement for the High Priest before offering national sacrifices. The High Priest, in making the offering for the nation, must first offer a goat for atonement of his own sins before God could accept the sacrifice of the people.

God does not require any less of us today than He did of the Israelites 4,000 years ago. When reading these passages do not focus on the performance of the rites, look at why they were required. These admonitions are still required of us today.

- We are to set aside times to celebrate and praise God.
- We are to come before God with a contrite heart offering ourselves in repentance.
- We are to set aside times to make offerings for God.
- We are to set aside times to offer thanks for special gifts from God.
- We are to set aside times to remember who we are and who God is.

The greatness of this new covenant is that when we come before God the purification sacrifice has already been offered once and for all and we approach God with our High Priest who is spotless and without blemish.

GOAL:

A veil, a High Priest and a sacrifice. They touched the lives of the Jews and influenced their relationship with God. Their spiritual counterparts are to touch our lives and influence our relationship with God. You are encouraged to define the veil, recognize the reverence required when going before God for atonement, and honor and prize the one-time sacrifice of Jesus and the freedom that gives you. What I have covered in this chapter is just a scraping of the surface. Many hours can be spent finding correlations throughout the Bible, allowing you to discover the joy and satisfaction of putting several more pieces of life's puzzle together.

Scripture Reference:

[44] Hebrews 10:10

XIII

Abraham:

The Friend Of God

"And the scripture was fulfilled that says, "Abraham believed God, and it was credited to him as righteousness," and he was called God's friend." — James 2:23

You see a neighbor outside in his backyard everyday digging, hoeing and pulling weeds. You feel sorry for him and want to help, but he says he is fine, thanks anyway. As the days go by your feelings of compassion grow, so you find another friend who owns a tiller and borrow it from him. The next morning you arise early and place the tiller right in the middle of the patch of ground your neighbor has been working on. As the day goes by you listen for the sound of the tiller at work but never hear anything. You peek over the fence and see your neighbor digging up the earth with a shovel. The tiller is still right where you left it, leaving you a bit surprised and somewhat dismayed. Then you question yourself; maybe he does not know how to use the tiller. So you call over the fence and ask why he is not using the tiller. He replies that he appreciates the thought but he is doing the work by hand as exercise to benefit his health and also as a tribute to his late wife. He explains that she always wanted to be able to look out at a flower garden from her bedroom window. It was not that your neighbor did not appreciate what you had done for him; on any other occasion, he said, he would have used your gift.

Abram had received a promise from a friend that he would be blessed with a family. At the ripe old age of 85, though, he was worried about how that promise was going to be kept. After discussions with his wife, he took a young servant and had relations with her and fathered a son. His intentions were good. He was just trying to help out a friend. It was not a lack of faith in his friend; even more so, it was a desire to honor his friend.

Abram's friend returned and told him that his actions were misguided. Then a promise was given that within a year his blessing would be fulfilled. Finally, at the age of 100, Abram welcomed the first child to his family and a new nation was born out of the promise.

As God's friend, the newly renamed Abraham was honored and respected by his neighbors and enemies. As God's friend Abraham followed Him wherever He went. As God's friend he permitted Lot to make the decision where to live. As God's friend he mediated between Sarah and Hagar. As God's friend he was introduced to a priest named Melchizedek. As God's friend he lived in a land of promise and was witness to the beginning of the nation his friend had promised. As God's friend he was at peace and became one of the most honored and revered men in all of history. As God's friend Abraham's shortcomings and vanity were tolerated and his strengths and virtues broadcast. The good points about God's friends are much more important to Him than their bad points.

God has many friends. Not all are famous. Not all are wealthy. Not all live in nice homes. Not all have many friends and few enemies. Not all live a life with little or no conflict. But all of God's friends do enjoy these things: All are living a life of promise. All are at peace within themselves. All have a relationship with God. All look forward to their home of promise. All enjoy being with God's friends. All want everyone to become God's friend.

The story of Abraham can be found in Genesis 11:26 – Genesis 24:2 and Genesis 25:1-10. Beyond these passages of scripture, Abraham's name is mentioned more than 140 times throughout the Bible.

Jesus had a lot to say about Abraham throughout the New Testament, including Luke 16:19-31; Luke 19:9; John 8:31-40 and John 8:52-58. We will not go into detail with these passages, but I find it interesting that some of the most troublesome passages for the Jews back then and for us today are these concerning Abraham.

Why? Because there are so many questions that arise from these stories. So many people have developed beliefs and centered their faith on what they think these passages are saying. Most people read them and turn away because these words either challenge a current belief or challenge them to form their own belief, which they do not want to do. Some turn away from fear, some from laziness, and some because they do not care what the Scripture says.

These are questions and challenges that every Christian will have to face somewhere along the road to maturity and intimacy with God. If they are still an enigma to you, then understand that God is not finished with you yet and you have a way to go. Continue on with your studies and walk with God and He will bring you back to these passages when you are more prepared. That is how God works with His friends.

Jesus' discourse on friendship and the life examples of Abraham are how we can know and see how God and His friends interact. Read John 15:9-15 and see that Jesus has chosen you to be His friend. He loves you. You will show Him and the world that you are His friend by your love for Him.

How do you show your friendship? Make a list of how you have shown and shared your friendship with others.

What are you doing to show the world that you are a friend of God and Jesus? Make a list of ways you are showing the world that Jesus is your friend.

GOAL:

My goal is to encourage each of you to continue building an intimate friendship with God and Jesus, realizing that it may not come easy and it will entail giving up much of self. But take God's word and that of His friends, it is worth it. Abraham was not perfect. He made some pretty big mistakes but God took Abraham's vainness and turned it into a blessing with Abimelech. What dark blot do you have in your life that God can turn into light in your life? What weakness do you have to struggle with that God can turn into a strength? What promise has God made to you that requires you to develop an even deeper faith while waiting for the promise to be fulfilled? I have prayed on many occasions for help in overcoming weaknesses. God has promised that He will help me overcome them. Some were overcome fairly quickly and easily but others are still being worked on after years. But know this; God will see that I do overcome them because He is a faithful friend who keeps His promises. God has made the same promise to you but it is not an easy way out. He has never promised you will not have to pay the consequences of wrongdoings in this life. What He has promised is that He will be with you, support you and give you peace until the day Jesus returns and takes us to glory. He also says that He believes in you[45]. Now that is a friend!

Scripture Reference:

[45] Isaiah 26:3

Conclusion

My prayer as you use this book to study God's Word is that you get excited about what is in the Bible and you have decided to go to The Good Book for answers to the questions you have about life. In the Introduction you were promised a method or way of studying the Scriptures on your own.

But first, why include all the genealogies, repetitiveness, census numbers, and other seemingly inconsequential details and then omit some of the important details that would remove some of the mystery in some passages? To be absolutely accurate, only God can answer these questions. I learned more about God in these passages and believe they are here for us to see how God works and what he wants us to get to know about Him. He is meticulous, He does not miss anything that happens in our life, He wants us to slow down at times and pay attention to details, nothing that happens is too small for Him to notice, and He will insert comments inside these lists to prick our interests and challenge us with a perception that we may have that needs correcting. Teachers and educators have always emphasized repetition. The way we learned the multiplication tables, the way we memorize Scripture, or anything else for that matter, is through repetition. And, one more point. In Abraham's story in Genesis it says Abram chose 318 men to go with him to fight a battle. In other sections of the Bible the years seem to be rounded off (the use of the number 40 in describing events and time periods of people's lives). God uses these numbers and lists to remind us that some things are meant to be exact and detailed while others are there to help us grasp the big picture, which in a particular case is more important than the details. When we start seeing how and why God uses a particular form in describing an event or supplying a list, we begin to know a little bit more about Him.

So here now are my approaches to reading and studying the Bible. Read, read, read. Get in the habit. Do whatever it takes to develop a thirst for reading God's Word. There are many Bibles and booklets for reading through the Bible in one year. A variation on that is reading the narrated Bible — one in which the Bible is laid out chronologically — in a year. In that version, the books of prophecy are intermixed with Kings and Chronicles so that you know what was going on in Israel when the prophets were making prophecies. The gospels are intermixed to help you walk through Jesus' life from birth to death to ascension. Appendix A is taken from one of these narrated versions.

I prefer to read the Bible in sections. I will choose a book or passage and read it through, sometimes two or three times over a month or more. I take notes on interesting passages or passages I think I have heard somewhere else or that stir some other idea. I set these notes aside until I have finished with the section.

Another Bible study method is reading to help me if I am unusually angry, moody, sad, happy or excited. I go to passages that will comfort, calm or lift me. Many times I go straight to the Psalms but just as often I read about certain characters and what kind of life they lived and how they found their most critical answers in God.

I also enjoy just picking up the Bible, opening it, and reading it from wherever I am. It still amazes me how many times I find an application in these verses that help me through a current situation in my life. This often happens when I purposely develop areas I want to study.

After developing a reading habit it becomes a natural progression to move into studying. Of course you do not have to wait for the reading to become a daily event before you begin studying. If I had waited for that, I would probably have never gotten around to studying. After a while reading and studying feed off each other; you read as part of your study and you study because of something you read.

Now, how to go about studying. I go back to notes I have been compiling or go right from reading a passage into studying it. Many times my study is dictated by a Bible class I am leading or a sermon I am scheduled to deliver. I am also often asked to help explain passages of scripture or doctrinal issues for someone so I will research and study the subject and present them with my findings. I also study to help me overcome weaknesses in my life or in my understanding of scripture.

For your computer or smart phone I strongly recommend one of the software packages that have several versions of the Bible, one or more concordances (including a topical one), Bible dictionary, maps and commentaries. If you do not have a computer with internet or a smart phone, then a good analytical concordance for the Bible translation you are reading plus a Bible dictionary with maps are of great help.

For instance in Chapter I we looked at Joseph. A concordance will list every time the name Joseph is used in the Scriptures. You need to insure that the Scriptures you will be using for your study are only about that particular subject. For this chapter I divided Joseph's life up into the events described in Genesis. I then went to the gospels (Matthew, Mark, Luke and John) to find events in Jesus' life that paralleled those in Joseph's. Finally, I looked at my own life and found events that paralleled those in the lives of Joseph and Jesus. For Chapter II I remembered the story of Moses from childhood and read it in Exodus, but I had never tied it together with Stephen's account in Acts. By doing so and noticing where Stephen put the emphasis in his narrative, I saw a different picture than what I had accepted for years. While combining the two passages, events from the life of Jesus kept coming to mind, so I would go to the gospels and find the parallels. You can easily spend six to eight hours in a study of this type.

I had always wondered why a man like Samson was honored so in the book of Judges. Many times I had read the passage in Hebrews 11 concerning his faith, but I never made the connection until I decided to discover why God had honored such a man. Studying some of the words and learning their usage and definition when they were written helped put some passages into perspective. For this I used Vine's and Strong's Concordance. By reading and rereading the passages and talking to God about them, I believe I came to see Samson as God saw him. You could complete a study like this in two to three hours.

I will also use an interlinear Bible to read the literal translation of the Greek and Hebrew words so I can see how the passage was originally written. If you know Greek or Hebrew you are at a distinct advantage in this area.

I use commentaries in one of two ways. One way is to get me jump started on a subject when I really do not know where to start. This happened much more frequently in my early days of learning to study. Or, it could be when I am tackling a difficult doctrinal issue. This helps me to see if the commentaries are reflecting the same thing in the passage that I am seeing. I try to never let the commentary tell me what God is saying in a passage of Scripture. I will discuss the passage with God, then take what the commentary has said and ask His Spirit to guide me in understanding and applying the passage. I will also discuss with others the passage and its meaning. Many Scriptures will say different things to different people depending on where they are in their life relationships, situations and maturity. Many Scriptures will have more than one application. This is especially true as you grow in knowledge, stature and wisdom.

I believe this about Bible study. You gain knowledge from yourself when you study the Bible. You gain wisdom when you include God and His Spirit and this wisdom leads to reaping the benefits of a strengthened and maturing spiritual life. What I am saying is that someone with a vast amount of knowledge does not necessarily have any more wisdom than one who has just begun learning about God and His Word. Do not leave God and the Holy Spirit out of your reading and study!

Lastly, trust God and the Holy Spirit to lead you into a full understanding of who you are and who He wants you to be. Get comfortable talking and listening to Him. To explain how you listen to God is impossible for me to do because He may talk to you in a different way than He does to me. Throughout the Old Testament He talked to man in many different ways:

From a burning bush[46]

As a donkey[47]

Through angels[48-53]

In dreams[54-56]

Through visions[57-58]

Today He talks to us in many ways through His Word. As you grow in wisdom and stature you will discover these ways and be amazed and thrilled, because God talks to His friends and when you learn to listen, you are a friend of God! May the Lord bless you and keep you until you have been given the place prepared by Jesus for you.

Amen.

Scripture References:

[46] Exodus 3:2-4

[47] Numbers 22:32-33

[48] Genesis 16:7

[49] Genesis 19:1

[50] Genesis 22:11

[51] Judges 2:4

[52] Judges 6:12

[53] Daniel 6:21

[54] Genesis 28:12

[55] 1 Kings 3:5

[56] Daniel 2:26-28

[57] Isaiah 1:1

[58] Ezekiel 1:1

Appendix A

The Last 18 Hours of
Jesus the Christ's Life
Before Dying On The Cross

(This passage is taken from *The Narrated Bible* by F. LaGard Smith, Harvest House Publishers, 1984.)

When the hour came, Jesus and his apostles reclined at the table. And he said to them, *"I have eagerly desired to eat this Passover with you before I suffer. For I tell you, I will not eat it again until it finds fulfillment in the kingdom of God."*

After taking the cup, he gave thanks and said, *"Take this and divide it among you. For I tell you I will not drink again of the fruit of the vine until the kingdom of God comes."*

And he took the bread, gave thanks and broke it, and gave it to them saying, *"This is my body given for you; do this in remembrance of me."*

In the same way, after the supper he took the cup, saying, "This cup is the new covenant in my blood, which is poured out for you."

"But the hand of him who is going to betray me is with mine on the table." They began to question among themselves which of them it might be who would do this.

Also a dispute arose among them as to which of them was considered to be greatest. Jesus said to them, *"The kings of the Gentiles lord it over them; and those who exercise authority over them call themselves Benefactors. But you are not to be like that. Instead, the greatest among you should be like the youngest, and the one who rules like the one who serves. You are those who have stood by me in my trials. And I confer on you a kingdom, just as my Father conferred one on me, so that you may eat and drink at my table in my kingdom and sit on thrones, judging the twelve tribes of Israel."*

Jesus knew that the time had come for him to leave this world and go to the Father. Having loved his own who were in the world, he now showed them the full extent of his love.

The evening meal was being served, and the devil had already prompted Judas Iscariot, son of Simon, to betray Jesus. Jesus knew that the Father had put all things under his power, and that he had come from God and was returning to God; so he got up from the meal, took off his outer clothing, and wrapped a towel around his waist. After that, he poured water into a basin and began to wash his disciples' feet, drying them with a towel that was wrapped around him.

He came to Simon Peter, who said to him, "Lord, are you going to wash my feet?"

Jesus replied *"You do not realize now what I am doing, but later you will understand."*

"No," said Peter, "you shall never wash my feet."

Jesus answered, *"Unless I wash you, you have no part with me."*

"Then, Lord," Simon Peter replied, "not just my feet but my hands and my head as well."

Jesus answered, *"A person who has had a bath needs only wash his feet; his whole body is clean. And you are clean, though not every one of you."* For he knew who was going to betray him, and that was why he said not everyone was clean.

When he had finished washing their feet, he put on his clothes and returned to his place. *"Do you understand what I have done for you?"* he asked them. *"You call me 'Teacher' and 'Lord', and rightly so, for that is what I am. Now that I, your Lord and Teacher, have washed your feet, you also should wash one another's feet. I have set you an example that you should do as I have done for you. I tell you the truth, no servant is greater than his master, nor is a messenger greater than the one who sent him. Now that you know these things, you will be blessed if you do them.*

"I am not referring to all of you; I know those I have chosen. But this is to fulfill the scripture: 'He who shares my bread has lifted up his heel against me'.

"I am telling you now before it happens, so that when it does happen you will believe that I am He. I tell you the truth, whoever

accepts anyone I send accepts me; and whoever accepts me accepts the one who sent me."

After he said this, Jesus was troubled in spirit and testified, *"I tell you the truth, one of you is going to betray me."*

They were very sad and began to say to him one after the other, "Surely not I, Lord?"

Jesus replied, *"The one who has dipped his hand into the bowl with me will betray me. The Son of Man will go just as it is written about him. But woe to that man who betrays the Son of Man! It would be better for him if he had not been born."* His disciples stared at one another, at a loss to know which of them he meant. One of them, the disciple whom Jesus loved, was reclining next to him. Simon Peter motioned to this disciple and said, "Ask him which one he means."

Leaning back against Jesus, he asked him, "Lord, who is it?"

Jesus answered, *"It is the one to whom I will give this piece of bread, when I have dipped it into the dish."* Then, dipping the piece of bread, he gave it to Judas Iscariot, son of Simon. As soon as Judas took the bread, Satan entered into him. Then Judas, the one who would betray him, said, "Surely, not I, Rabbi?"

Jesus answered, *"Yes, it is you.*

"What you are about to do, do quickly," Jesus told him, but no one at the meal understood why Jesus said this to him. Since Judas had charge of the money, some thought Jesus was telling him to buy what was needed for the Feast, or to give something to the

poor. As soon as Judas had taken the bread, he went out. And it was night.

When he was gone, Jesus said, *"Now is the Son of Man glorified and God is glorified in him. If God is glorified in him, God will glorify the Son in himself, and will glorify him at once.*

"My children, I will be with you only a little longer. You will look for me, and just as I told the Jews, so I tell you now: Where I am going, you cannot come.

"A new command I give you: Love one another. As I have loved you, so you must love one another. By this all men will know that you are my disciples, if you love one another."

Simon Peter asked him, "Lord, where are you going?"

Jesus replied, *"Where I am going, you cannot follow now, but you will follow later."*

Peter asked, "Lord, why can't I follow you now? I will lay down my life for you. *"Simon, Simon, Satan has asked to sift you as wheat. But I have prayed for you, Simon, that your faith may not fail. And when you have turned back, strengthen your brothers."*

But he replied, "Lord, I am ready to go with you to prison and to death."

Jesus answered, *"I tell you, Peter, before the rooster crows today, you will deny three times that you know me.*

Do not let your hearts be troubled. Trust in God; trust also in me. In my Father's house are many rooms; if it were not so, I would have told you. I am going there to prepare a place for you. And if I go and prepare a place for you, I will come back and take you to be

117

with me that you also may be where I am. You know the way to the place I am going."

Thomas said to him, "Lord, we don't know where you are going, so how can we know the way?"

Jesus answered, *"I am the way and the truth and the life. No one comes to the Father except through me. If you really knew me, you would know my Father as well. From now on, you do know him and have seen him."*

Philip said, "Lord, show us the Father and that will be enough for us."

Jesus answered, *"Don't you know me, Philip, even after I have been among you such a long time? Anyone who has seen me has seen the Father. How can you say, 'Show us the Father'? Don't you believe that I am in the Father, and that the Father is in me? The words I say to you are not just my own. Rather, it is the Father, living in me, who is doing his work. Believe me when I say that I am in the Father and the Father is in me; or at least believe on the evidence of the miracles themselves. I tell you the truth, anyone who has faith in me will do what I have been doing. He will do even greater things than these, because I am going to the Father. And I will do whatever you ask in my name, so that the Son may bring glory to the Father. You may ask me for anything in my name, and I will do it.*

"If you love me, you will obey what I command.

"And I will ask the Father, and he will give you another Counselor to be with you forever—the Spirit of truth. The world

cannot accept him, because it neither sees him nor knows him. But you know him, for he lives with you and will be in you. I will not leave you as orphans; I will come to you. Before long, the world will not see me anymore, but you will see me. Because I live, you also will live. On that day you will realize that I am in my Father, and you are in me, and I am in you. Whoever has my commands and obeys them, he is the one who loves me. He who loves me will be loved by my Father, and I too will love him and show myself to him."

Then Judas (not Judas Iscariot) said, "But, Lord, why do you intend to show yourself to us and not to the world?"

Jesus replied, *"If anyone loves me, he will obey my teaching. My Father will love him, and we will come to him and make our home with him. He who does not love me will not obey my teaching. These words you hear are not my own; they belong to the Father who sent me.*

"All this I have spoken while still with you. But the Counselor, the Holy Spirit, whom the Father will send in my name, will teach you all things and will remind you of everything I have said to you. Peace I leave with you; my peace I give you. I do not give to you as the world gives. Do not let your hearts be troubled and do not be afraid.

"You heard me say, 'I am going away and I am coming back to you.' If you loved me, you would be glad that I am going to the Father, for the Father is greater than I. I have told you now before it happens, so that when it does happen you will believe. I will not speak with you much longer, for the prince of this world is coming.

He has no hold on me, but the world must learn that I love the Father and that I do exactly what my Father has commanded me." Then Jesus asked them, *"When I sent you without purse, bag or sandals, did you lack anything?"*

"Nothing," they answered.

He said to them, *"But now if you have a purse, take it, and also a bag; and if you don't have a sword, sell your cloak and buy one. It is written: 'And he was numbered with the transgressors'; and I tell you that this must be fulfilled in me. Yes, what is written about me is reaching its fulfillment."*

The disciples said, "See, Lord, here are two swords."

"That is enough," he replied.

"Come now let us leave."

When they had sung a hymn, they went out to the Mount of Olives.

Then Jesus told them, *"This very night you will all fall away on account of me, for it is written: "'I will strike the shepherd, and the sheep of the flock will be scattered.' But after I have risen, I will go ahead of you into Galilee."*

Peter replied, "Even if all fall away on account of you, I never will."

"I tell you the truth," Jesus answered, *"this very night, before the rooster crows, you will disown me three times."*

But Peter declared, "Even if I have to die with you, I will never disown you." And all the other disciples said the same.

"I am the true vine, and my Father is the gardener. He cuts off every branch in me that bears no fruit, while every branch that does bear fruit he prunes so that it will be even more fruitful. You are already clean because of the word I have spoken to you. Remain in me, and I will remain in you. No branch can bear fruit by itself; it must remain in the vine. Neither can you bear fruit unless you remain in me. "I am the vine; you are the branches. If a man remains in me and I in him, he will bear much fruit; apart from me you can do nothing. If anyone does not remain in me, he is like a branch that is thrown away and withers; such branches are picked up, thrown into the fire and burned. If you remain in me and my words remain in you, ask whatever you wish, and it will be given you. This is to my Father's glory, that you bear much fruit, showing yourselves to be my disciples.

"As the Father has loved me, so have I loved you. Now remain in my love. If you obey my commands, you will remain in my love, just as I have obeyed my Father's commands and remain in his love. I have told you this so that my joy may be in you and that your joy may be complete. My command is this: Love each other as I have loved you. Greater love has no one than this, that he lay down his life for his friends. You are my friends if you do what I command. I no longer call you servants, because a servant does not know his master's business. Instead, I have called you friends, for everything that I learned from my Father I have made known to you. You did not choose me, but I chose you and appointed you to go and bear

fruit-- fruit that will last. Then the Father will give you whatever you ask in my name. This is my command: Love each other.

"If the world hates you, keep in mind that it hated me first. If you belonged to the world, it would love you as its own. As it is, you do not belong to the world, but I have chosen you out of the world. That is why the world hates you. Remember the words I spoke to you: 'No servant is greater than his master.' If they persecuted me, they will persecute you also. If they obeyed my teaching, they will obey yours also. They will treat you this way because of my name, for they do not know the One who sent me. If I had not come and spoken to them, they would not be guilty of sin. Now, however, they have no excuse for their sin. He who hates me hates my Father as well. If I had not done among them what no one else did, they would not be guilty of sin. But now they have seen these miracles, and yet they have hated both me and my Father. But this is to fulfill what is written in their Law: 'They hated me without reason.'

"When the Counselor comes, whom I will send to you from the Father, the Spirit of truth who goes out from the Father, he will testify about me. And you also must testify, for you have been with me from the beginning.

"All this I have told you so that you will not go astray. They will put you out of the synagogue; in fact, a time is coming when anyone who kills you will think he is offering a service to God. They will do such things because they have not known the Father or me. I have told you this, so that when the time comes you will remember

that I warned you. I did not tell you this at first because I was with you.

"Now I am going to him who sent me, yet none of you asks me, 'Where are you going?'

"Because I have said these things, you are filled with grief. But I tell you the truth: It is for your good that I am going away. Unless I go away, the Counselor will not come to you; but if I go, I will send him to you. When he comes, he will convict the world of guilt in regard to sin and righteousness and judgment: in regard to sin, because men do not believe in me; in regard to righteousness, because I am going to the Father, where you can see me no longer; and in regard to judgment, because the prince of this world now stands condemned.

"I have much more to say to you, more than you can now bear. But when he, the Spirit of truth, comes, he will guide you into all truth. He will not speak on his own; he will speak only what he hears, and he will tell you what is yet to come. He will bring glory to me by taking from what is mine and making it known to you. All that belongs to the Father is mine. That is why I said the Spirit will take from what is mine and make it known to you.

"In a little while you will see me no more, and then after a little while you will see me."

Some of his disciples said to one another, "What does he mean by saying, 'In a little while you will see me no more, and then after a little while you will see me,' and 'Because I am going to the

Father'?" They kept asking, "What does he mean by 'a little while'? We don't understand what he is saying."

Jesus saw that they wanted to ask him about this, so he said to them, *"Are you asking one another what I meant when I said, 'In a little while you will see me no more, and then after a little while you will see me'? I tell you the truth, you will weep and mourn while the world rejoices. You will grieve, but your grief will turn to joy. A woman giving birth to a child has pain because her time has come; but when her baby is born she forgets the anguish because of her joy that a child is born into the world. So with you: Now is your time of grief, but I will see you again and you will rejoice, and no one will take away your joy. In that day you will no longer ask me anything. I tell you the truth, my Father will give you whatever you ask in my name. Until now you have not asked for anything in my name. Ask and you will receive, and your joy will be complete.*

Then Jesus' disciples said, "Now you are speaking clearly and without figures of speech. Now we can see that you know all things and that you do not even need to have anyone ask you questions. This makes us believe that you came from God."

"You believe at last!" Jesus answered. *"But a time is coming, and has come, when you will be scattered, each to his own home. You will leave me all alone. Yet I am not alone, for my Father is with me.*

"I have told you these things, so that in me you may have peace. In this world you will have trouble. But take heart! I have overcome the world."

After Jesus said this, he looked toward heaven and prayed: *"Father, the time has come. Glorify your Son, that your Son may glorify you. For you granted him authority over all people that he might give eternal life to all those you have given him. Now this is eternal life: that they may know you, the only true God, and Jesus Christ, whom you have sent. I have brought you glory on earth by completing the work you gave me to do. And now, Father, glorify me in your presence with the glory I had with you before the world began.*

"I have revealed you to those whom you gave me out of the world. They were yours; you gave them to me and they have obeyed your word. Now they know that everything you have given me comes from you. For I gave them the words you gave me and they accepted them. They knew with certainty that I came from you, and they believed that you sent me. I pray for them. I am not praying for the world, but for those you have given me, for they are yours. All I have is yours, and all you have is mine. And glory has come to me through them. I will remain in the world no longer, but they are still in the world, and I am coming to you. Holy Father, protect them by the power of your name-- the name you gave me-- so that they may be one as we are one. While I was with them, I protected them and kept them safe by that name you gave me. None has been lost except the one doomed to destruction so that Scripture would be fulfilled.

"I am coming to you now, but I say these things while I am still in the world, so that they may have the full measure of my joy within them. I have given them your word and the world has hated

them, for they are not of the world any more than I am of the world. My prayer is not that you take them out of the world but that you protect them from the evil one. They are not of the world, even as I am not of it. Sanctify them by the truth; your word is truth. As you sent me into the world, I have sent them into the world. For them I sanctify myself, that they too may be truly sanctified.

"My prayer is not for them alone. I pray also for those who will believe in me through their message, that all of them may be one, Father, just as you are in me and I am in you. May they also be in us so that the world may believe that you have sent me. I have given them the glory that you gave me, that they may be one as we are one: I in them and you in me. May they be brought to complete unity to let the world know that you sent me and have loved them even as you have loved me.

"Father, I want those you have given me to be with me where I am, and to see my glory, the glory you have given me because you loved me before the creation of the world.

"Righteous Father, though the world does not know you, I know you, and they know that you have sent me. I have made you known to them, and will continue to make you known in order that the love you have for me may be in them and that I myself may be in them."

When he had finished praying, Jesus left with his disciples and crossed the Kidron Valley. On the other side there was an olive grove, and he and his disciples went into it. They went to a place called Gethsemane, and Jesus said to his disciples, *"Sit here while I pray."* He took Peter, James and John along with him, and he began to be deeply distressed and troubled. *"My soul is overwhelmed with sorrow to the point of death,"* he said to them. *"Stay here and keep watch."*

He withdrew about a stone's throw beyond them, knelt down and prayed, *"Father, if you are willing, take this cup from me; yet not my will, but yours be done."* An angel from heaven appeared to him and strengthened him. And being in anguish, he prayed more earnestly, and his sweat was like drops of blood falling to the ground.

When he rose from prayer and went back to the disciples, he found them asleep, exhausted from sorrow.

Then he returned to his disciples and found them sleeping. *"Could you men not keep watch with me for one hour?"* he asked Peter. *"Watch and pray so that you will not fall into temptation. The spirit is willing, but the body is weak."* He went away a second time and prayed, *"My Father, if it is not possible for this cup to be taken away unless I drink it, may your will be done."*

When he came back, he again found them sleeping, because their eyes were heavy. So he left them and went away once more and prayed the third time, saying the same thing. Then he returned to the disciples and said to them, *"Are you still sleeping and resting? Look, the hour is near, and the Son of Man is betrayed into the hands of sinners. Rise, let us go! Here comes my betrayer!"*

Now Judas, who betrayed him, knew the place, because Jesus had often met there with his disciples. So Judas came to the grove, guiding a detachment of soldiers and some officials from the chief priests and Pharisees. They were carrying torches, lanterns and weapons. Just as he was speaking, Judas, one of the Twelve, appeared. With him was a crowd armed with swords and clubs, sent from the chief priests, the teachers of the law, and the elders. Now the betrayer had arranged a signal with them: "The one I kiss is the man; arrest him and lead him away under guard." While he was still speaking a crowd came up, and the man who was called Judas, one of the Twelve, was leading them. He approached Jesus to kiss him, but Jesus asked him, *"Judas, are you betraying the Son of Man with a kiss?"* Going at once to Jesus, Judas said, "Rabbi!" and kissed him.

Jesus, knowing all that was going to happen to him, went out and asked them, *"Who is it you want?"* "Jesus of Nazareth," they replied. *"I am he,"* Jesus said. (And Judas the traitor was standing there with them.) When Jesus said, *"I am he,"* they drew back and fell to the ground. Again he asked them, *"Who is it you want?"* And they said, "Jesus of Nazareth."

"I told you that I am he," Jesus answered. *"If you are looking for me, then let these men go."* This happened so that the words he had spoken would be fulfilled: "I have not lost one of those you gave me."

The men seized Jesus and arrested him. When Jesus' followers saw what was going to happen, they said, "Lord should we strike with our swords?" Then Simon Peter, who had a sword, drew it and struck the high priest's servant, cutting off his right ear. (The servant's name was Malchus.) *"Put your sword back in its place,"*

Jesus said to him, *"for all who draw the sword will die by the sword. Do you think I cannot call on my Father, and he will at once put at my disposal more than twelve legions of angels? But how then would the scriptures be fulfilled that say it must happen in this way?"*

Then Jesus said to the chief priests, the officers of the temple guard, and the elders, who had come for him, *"Am I leading a rebellion, that you have come with swords and clubs? Every day I was with you in the temple courts, and you did not lay a hand on me. But this is your hour—when darkness reigns."*

Then the detachment of soldiers with its commander and the Jewish officials arrested Jesus. Then all the disciples deserted and fled. A young man, wearing nothing but a linen garment, was following Jesus. When they seized him, he fled naked, leaving his garment behind.

They bound him and brought him first to Annas, who was the father-in-law of Caiaphas, the high priest that year. Caiaphas was the one who had advised the Jews that it would be good if one man died for the people.

Simon Peter and another disciple were following Jesus. Because this disciple was known to the high priest, he went with Jesus into the high priest's courtyard, but Peter had to wait outside at the door. The other disciple, who was known to the high priest, came back, spoke to the girl on duty there and brought Peter in. "You are not one of the man's disciples, are you?" the girl at the door asked Peter. He replied, "I am not."

Meanwhile, the high priest questioned Jesus about his disciples and his teaching.

"I have spoken openly to the world," Jesus replied. *"I always taught in synagogues or at the temple, where all the Jews come together. I said nothing in secret. Why question me? Ask those who hear me. Surely they know what I said."*

When Jesus said this, one of the officials nearby struck him in the face. "Is this the way you answer the high priest?" he demanded.

"If I said something wrong," Jesus replied, *"testify as to what is wrong. But if I spoke the truth, why did you strike me?"*

Then Annas sent him, still bound, to Caiaphas the high priest. Then seizing, him, they led him away and took him into the house of the high priest. Peter followed at a distance.

But when they had kindled a fire in the middle of the courtyard and had sat down together, Peter sat down with them. A servant girl saw him seated there in the firelight. She looked closely at him and said, "This man was with him."

But he denied it. "Woman, I don't know him," he said. Then he went out to the gateway, where another girl saw him and said to the people, "This fellow was with Jesus of Nazareth."

He denied it again, with an oath: "I don't know the man!" A little later someone else saw him and said, "You also are one of them."

"Man, I am not!" Peter replied.

The chief priests and the whole Sanhedrin were looking for evidence against Jesus so that they could put him to death, but they did not find any. Many testified falsely against him but their statements did not agree.

Then some stood up and gave this false testimony against him: "We heard him say, 'I will destroy this man-made temple and in three days will build another, not made by man.'" Yet even then their testimony did not agree.

Again the high priest asked him, "Are you the Christ, the Son of the Blessed One?"

"I am," said Jesus. *"And you will see the Son of Man sitting at the right hand of the Mighty One and coming on the clouds of heaven."*

The high priest tore his clothes. "Why do we need any more witnesses?" he asked. "You have heard the blasphemy. What do you think?"

They all condemned him as worthy of death.

The men who were guarding Jesus began mocking and beating him. They blindfolded him and demanded, "Prophesy! Who hit you?" And they said many other insulting things to him.

After a little while (about an hour later), those standing there went up to Peter and said "Surely you are one of them, for your accent gives you away."

Then he began to call down curses on himself and he swore to them, "I don't know the man!" One of the high priest's servants, a relative of the man whose ear Peter had cut off, challenged him,

"Didn't I see you with him in the olive grove?" Peter replied, "Man, I don't know what you're talking about!"

Just as he was speaking, the rooster crowed. The Lord turned and looked straight at Peter. Then Peter remembered the word the Lord had spoken to him: *"Before the rooster crows today, you will disown me three times."* And he went outside and wept bitterly.

At daybreak the council of the elders of the people, both the chief priests and teachers of the law, met together, and Jesus was led before them. "If you are the Christ," they said, "tell us."

Jesus answered, *"If I tell you, you will not believe me, and if I asked you, you would not answer. But from now on, the Son of Man will be seated at the right hand of the mighty God."*

They all asked, "Are you then the Son of God?"

He replied, *"You are right in saying I am."*

Then they said, "Why do we need any more testimony? We have heard it from his own lips." Early in the morning, all the chief priests and the elders of the people came to the decision to put Jesus to death.

When Judas, who had betrayed him, saw that Jesus was condemned, he was seized with remorse and returned the thirty silver coins to the chief priests and the elders. "I have sinned," he said, "for I have betrayed innocent blood."

"What is that to us?" they replied. "That's your responsibility."

So Judas threw the money into the temple and left. Then he went away and hanged himself.

The chief priests picked up the coins and said, "It is against the law to put this into the treasury, since it is blood money." So they decided to use the money to buy the potter's field as a burial place for foreigners. That is why it has been called the Field of Blood to this day. Then what was spoken by Jeremiah the prophet was fulfilled: "They took the thirty pieces of silver coins, the price set on him by the people of Israel, and they used them to buy the potter's field, as the Lord commanded me."

They bound him, led him away and handed him over to Pilate, the governor. By now it was early morning, and to avoid ceremonial uncleanness the Jews did not enter the palace; they wanted to be able to eat the Passover. So Pilate came out to them and asked, "What charges are you bringing against this man?"

If he were not a criminal," they replied, "we would not have handed him over to you." And they began to accuse him, saying "We have found this man subverting our nation. He opposes payment of taxes to Caesar and claims to be Christ, a king." Pilate said, "Take him yourselves and judge him by your own law."

"But we have no right to execute anyone," the Jews objected. This happened so that the words Jesus had spoken indicating the kind of death he was going to die would be fulfilled.

Pilate then went back inside the palace, summoned Jesus and asked him, "Are you the king of the Jews?"

"Is that your own idea," Jesus asked, *"or did others talk to you about me?"*

"Am I a Jew?" Pilate replied. "It was your people and your chief priests who handed you over to me. What is it you have done?"

Jesus said, *"My kingdom is not of this world. If it were, my servants would fight to prevent my arrest by the Jews. But now my kingdom is from another place."*

"You are a king, then!" said Pilate.

Jesus answered, *"You are right in saying I am a king. In fact, for this reason I was born, and for this I came into the world, to testify to the truth. Everyone on the side of truth listens to me."*

"What is truth?" Pilate asked. With this he went out again to the Jews and said, "I find no basis for a charge against him." When he was accused by the chief priests and the elders, he gave no answer. Then Pilate asked him, "Don't you hear the testimony they are bringing against you?" But Jesus made no reply, not even to a single charge—to the great amazement of the governor.

"But they insisted, "He stirs up the people all over Judea by his teaching. He started in Galilee and has come all the way here."

On hearing this, Pilate asked if the man was a Galilean. When he learned that Jesus was under Herod's jurisdiction, he sent him to Herod, who was also in Jerusalem at that time.

When Herod saw Jesus, he was greatly pleased, because for a long time he had been wanting to see him. From what he had heard about him, he hoped to see him perform some miracle. He plied him with many questions, but Jesus gave him no answer. The chief priests and the teachers of the law were standing there, vehemently accusing him. Then Herod and his soldiers ridiculed and mocked him. Dressing him in an elegant robe, they sent him back to Pilate. That day Herod and Pilate became friends—before this they had been enemies.

While Pilate was sitting on the judge's seat, his wife sent him this message: "Don't have anything to do with that innocent man, for I have suffered a great deal today in a dream because of him."

Pilate called together the chief priests, the rulers and the people, and said to them, "You brought me this man as one who was inciting the people to rebellion. I have examined him in your presence and have found no basis for your charges against him. Neither has Herod, for he sent him back to us; as you can see, he has done nothing to deserve death. Therefore, I will punish him and then release him."

Now it was the custom at the Feast to release a prisoner whom the people requested. A man called Barabbas was in prison with the insurrectionists who had committed murder in the uprising. The crowd came up and asked Pilate to do for them what he usually did.

"Do you want me to release to you the king of the Jews?" asked Pilate, knowing it was out of envy that the chief priests had handed Jesus over to them.

But the chief priests stirred up the crowd to have Pilate release Barabbas instead. They shouted back, "No, not him! Give us Barabbas!" With one voice they cried out, "Away with this man! Release Barabbas to us!" "Which of the two do you want me to release to you?" asked the governor.

"Barabbas," they answered.

"What shall I do, then, with Jesus who is called Christ?: Pilate asked.

They all answered, "Crucify him!"

"Why? What crime has he committed?" asked Pilate.

But they shouted all the louder, "Crucify him!" Wanting to release Jesus, Pilate appealed to them again. But they kept shouting, "Crucify him! Crucify him!"

For the third time he spoke to them: "Why? What crime has this man committed" I have found in him no grounds for the death penalty. Therefore I will have him punished and the release him."

But with loud shouts they insistently demanded that he be crucified, and their shouts prevailed.

Then Pilate took Jesus and had him flogged. Then the governor's soldiers took Jesus into the Praetorium and gathered the whole company of soldiers around him. They stripped him and put a scarlet robe on him, and then twisted together a crown of thorns and set it on his head. They put a staff in his right hand and knelt in front of him and mocked him. "Hail, king of the Jews!" they said. They spit on him, and took the staff and struck him on the head again and again.

Once more Pilate came out and said to the Jews, "Look, I am bringing him out to you to let you know that I find no basis for a charge against him." When Jesus came out wearing the crown of thorns and the purple robe, Pilate said to them, "Here is the man!"

As soon as the chief priests and their officials saw him, they shouted, "Crucify! Crucify!"

But Pilate answered, You take him and crucify him. As for me, I find no basis for a charge against him."

The Jews insisted, "We have a law, and according to that law he must die, because he claimed to be the Son of God."

When Pilate heard this, he was even more afraid, and he went back inside the palace. "Where do you come from?" he asked Jesus, but Jesus gave him no answer. "Do you refuse to speak to me?" Pilate said. "Don't you realize I have power either to free you or to crucify you?"

Jesus answered, *"You would have no power over me if it were not given to you from above. Therefore the one who handed me over to you is guilty of a greater sin."*

From then on, Pilate tried to set Jesus free, but the Jews kept shouting, "If you let this man go, you are no friend of Caesar. Anyone who claims to be a king opposes Caesar."

When Pilate heard this, he brought Jesus out and sat down on the judge's seat at a place known as the Stone Pavement (which in Aramaic is Gabbatha). It was the day of Preparation of Passover Week, about the sixth hour.

"Here is your king," Pilate said to the Jews.

But they shouted, "Take him away! Take him away! Crucify him!"

Shall I crucify your king?" Pilate asked.

"We have no king but Caesar," the chief priests answered.

When Pilate saw that he was getting nowhere, but that instead an uproar was starting, he took water and washed his hands in front of the crowd. "I am innocent of this man's blood," he said. "It is your responsibility!"

All the people answered, "Let his blood be on us and on our children!"

So Pilate decided to grant their demand. He released the man who had been thrown into prison for insurrection and murder, the one they asked for, and surrendered Jesus to their will.

And when they had mocked him, they took off the purple robe and put his own clothes on him. Then they led him out to crucify him. Carrying his own cross, he went out...

A certain man from Cyrene, Simon, the father of Alexander and Rufus, was passing by on his way in from the country, and they forced him to carry the cross. They brought Jesus to the place called Golgotha (which means The Place of the Skull).

A large number of people followed him, including women who mourned and wailed for him. Jesus turned and said to them, *"Daughters of Jerusalem, do not weep for me; weep for yourselves and for your children. For the time will come when you will say, 'Blessed are the barren women, the wombs that never bore and breasts that never nursed!' Then 'they will say to the mountains, "Fall on us!" and to the hills, "Cover us!"' For if men do these things when the tree is green, what will happen when it is dry?"*

Two other men, both criminals, were also led out with him to be executed. When they came to the place called the Skull, there they crucified him, along with the criminals—one on his right, the other on his left. Jesus said, *"Father, forgive them, for they do not know what they are doing."* Then they offered him wine mixed with myrrh, but he did not take it.

It was the third hour when they crucified him.

Pilate had a notice prepared and fastened to the cross. It read: JESUS OF NAZARETH, THE KING OF THE JEWS. Many of the Jews read this sign, for the place where Jesus was crucified was near the city, and the sign was written in Aramaic, Latin and Greek. The chief priests of the Jews protested to Pilate, "Do not write 'The King of the Jews', but that this man claimed to be king of the Jews."

Pilate answered, "What I have written, I have written."

When the soldiers crucified Jesus, they took his clothes, dividing them into four shares, one for each of them, with the undergarment remaining. This garment was seamless, woven in one piece from top to bottom.

"Let's not tear it," they said to one another. "Let's decide by lot who will get it."

This happened that the scripture might be fulfilled which said, "They divided my garments among them and cast lots for my clothing." So that is what the soldiers did.

Those who passed by hurled insults at him, shaking their heads and saying, "You who are going to destroy the temple and build it in three days, save yourself! Come down from the cross, if you are the Son of God!"

In the same way the chief priests, the teachers of the law and the elders mocked him, "He saved others," they said, "but he can't save himself. He's the King of Israel! Let him come down now from the cross, and we will believe in him. He trusts in God. Let God rescue him now if he wants him, for he said, 'I am the Son of God.'" The soldiers also came up and mocked him. They offered him wine vinegar and said, "If you are the king of the Jews, save yourself."

One of the criminals who hung there hurled insults at him: "Aren't you the Christ? Save yourself and us!"

But the other criminal rebuked him. "Don't you fear God," he said, "since you are under the same sentence? We are punished justly, for we are getting what our deeds deserve. But this man has done nothing wrong."

Then he said, "Jesus, remember me when you come into your kingdom."

Jesus answered him, *"I tell you the truth, today you will be with me in paradise."*

Near the cross of Jesus stood his mother, his mother's sister, Mary the wife of Clopas, and Mary Magdalene. When Jesus saw his mother there, and the disciple whom he loved standing nearby, he said to his mother, *"Dear woman, here is your son,"* and to the disciple, *"Here is your mother."* From that time on, this disciple took her into his home.

From the sixth hour until the ninth hour darkness came over all the land. About the ninth hour Jesus cried out in a loud voice,

"Eloi, Eloi, lama sabachthani?"— which means, *"My God, my God, why have you forsaken me?"*

When some of those standing there heard this, they said, "He's calling Elijah."

Later, knowing that all was now completed, and so that the Scripture would be fulfilled, Jesus said, *"I am thirsty."* Immediately one of them ran and got a sponge. He filled it with wine vinegar, put it on a stick, and offered it to Jesus to drink. The rest said, "Now leave him alone. Let's see if Elijah comes to save him."

When he had received the drink, Jesus said, *"It is finished."* Jesus called out with a loud voice, *"Father, into your hands I commit my spirit."* With that, he bowed his head and gave up his spirit.

Appendix B
Scripture References

1	2 Timothy 3:16-17	2	Acts 13:22
3	John 14:9	4	Luke 12:31
5	Colossians 3:13	6	2 Timothy 4:16
7	Romans 8:38, 39	8	Luke 6:28
9	John 14:6	10	Romans 5:8
11	Romans 8:35	12	2 Timothy 1:5
13	John 15:18	14	Acts 13:13
15	Hebrews 10:26	16	Matthew 5:14
17	Hosea 14:9	18	Ephesians 5:18
19	1 Corinthians 3:18-23	20	James 4:13-16
21	Luke 12:16-21	22	Romans 11:22
23	Ephesians 2:7	24	Titus 3:4-7
25	1 Corinthians 1:31	26	Ephesians 1:11
27	Romans 15:13-14	28	Titus 1:1-2
29	Luke 18:1	30	Hebrews 6:17-19
31	Matthew 7:7	32	Acts 17:27

33	Genesis 4:9	34	Matthew 25:40
35	Matthew 6:9-13	36	Jeremiah 31:31
37	John 14:16 (KJV, TLB)	38	1 John 4:16
39	1 John 4:8	40	Matthew 27:63-66
41	Genesis 2:24	42	Hebrews 13:8
43	Isaiah 1:18	44	Hebrews 10:10
45	Isaiah 26:3	46	Exodus 3:2-4
47	Numbers 22:32-33	48	Genesis 16:7
49	Genesis 19:1	50	Genesis 22:11
51	Judges 2:4	52	Judges 6:12
53	Daniel 6:21	54	Genesis 28:12
55	1 Kings 3:5	56	Daniel 2:26-28
57	Isaiah 1:1	58	Ezekiel 1:1

About Al Santymire

Al Santymire was born in North Carolina and grew up in rural West Virginia, about 70 miles west of Washington, DC. He preached his first sermon at the age of 10 when his mother and two brothers were snowed in on a Sunday and could not make it to church. As a teenager, Al was asked by a small Christian church to speak whenever the youth ministry hosted the evening service. Ever since those foundational days, Al has taken advantage of every opportunity to preach and teach God's Word.

Al has taught everyone from toddlers to adults and served as a church deacon in Campbell, CA for 12 years, also overseeing the Benevolence Ministry. Al currently serves as a Stephen Minister at 3Crosses in Castro Valley, CA and also volunteers for several other church ministries.

Al is available for speaking engagements and consulting through His Way Ministries. Please visit his website at www.iamyahweh.org.

Rick Chavez - Editor

Rick Chavez enjoyed a successful career as a Bay Area TV/Radio anchor and voiceover talent, interviewing Hall of Fame athletes, Olympic champions and Silicon Valley executives. He was Sports Director at NBC11 in San Jose and anchored at ABC7 and KRON4 in San Francisco.

Rick hosted Cisco's first international SMB webcast from The Netherlands. In addition, he anchored Oracle webcasts in New Orleans and San Diego. Rick produced Silicon Valley tech reports for CNBC-Europe, was the host of *"Best of the Bay"* and won four Telly Awards for broadcast and documentary production excellence.

Rick was Jubilee Bible College Valedictorian in 2011 and now specializes in writing for Christian and Senior Living audiences. He is available to work with other authors as a freelance editor, proofreader or publisher. Please contact chavezmedia@gmail.com.

www.ingramcontent.com/pod-product-compliance
Lightning Source LLC
Chambersburg PA
CBHW060156070426
42447CB00033B/1668